The Ultimate Pizza Cookbook

Dishes, Volume 3

Olivia Bennett

Published by B&H Publishing Group, 2025.

THE ULTIMATE PIZZA COOKBOOK

First edition. February 20, 2025.

ISBN: 979-8230166443

Written by Olivia Bennett.

Table of Contents

To everyone who believes that the best moments in life are shared over a slice of pizza.

To my family and friends, whose love and laughter have made every meal more special.

And to the passionate home cooks, pizza lovers, and kitchen adventurers who dare to knead, stretch, and top their way to perfection.

May your ovens stay hot, your crusts stay crispy, and your creativity never run out of toppings!

Introduction: A Slice of History

Few foods evoke as much universal love and passion as pizza. From its humble beginnings in Naples to its rise as a global culinary phenomenon, pizza has transcended cultural boundaries, becoming a staple in countless cuisines. Whether you enjoy a simple Margherita, a deep-dish Chicago-style pie, or an inventive gourmet creation, pizza's versatility and universal appeal make it a dish for all occasions.

In this chapter, we'll explore the fascinating history of pizza, discuss what makes it such a beloved food worldwide, and delve into why homemade pizza is the ultimate culinary experience. By understanding its roots and appreciating its evolution, you'll gain a deeper connection to the craft of pizza-making.

The Origins of Pizza

1. The Early Beginnings: Bread and Toppings

The concept of pizza—flatbread with toppings—dates back thousands of years. Early civilizations such as the Egyptians, Greeks, and Romans prepared flatbreads adorned with oils, herbs, and spices. These early "pizzas" were simple but provided the foundation for the dish we know today.

- Egyptians: The first recorded use of leavened bread.
- Greeks: Topped flatbreads with olive oil, herbs, and cheese, a dish known as "plakous."
- Romans: Created "focaccia," a flatbread often seasoned with olive oil and spices, paving the way for future pizza doughs.

2. The Birth of Modern Pizza in Naples

Modern pizza as we know it emerged in 18th-century Naples, Italy. It was initially a food for the poor, sold by street vendors and bakeries. These early pizzas were simple, affordable, and portable, making them an ideal meal for working-class Neapolitans.

- Tomato's Role: Tomatoes, introduced to Europe from the Americas in the 16th century, were initially thought to be poisonous. By the late 17th century, they became a staple in southern Italian cuisine, including pizza.

- First Pizza Vendors: Vendors sold pizza topped with tomatoes, garlic, and olive oil, creating the precursor to the modern pizza.

3. Margherita Pizza: A Royal Creation

In 1889, pizza took a significant leap toward global recognition when Queen Margherita of Savoy visited Naples. Chef Raffaele Esposito prepared a pizza featuring tomatoes, mozzarella, and basil to represent the colors of the Italian flag. This creation, now known as the Margherita pizza, brought legitimacy and prestige to what was once a humble street food.

4. Pizza's Journey to America

Italian immigrants brought pizza to the United States in the late 19th and early 20th centuries, where it quickly gained popularity in cities like New York and Chicago. By the mid-20th century, pizza had become a national favorite, thanks in part to returning World War II soldiers who had developed a taste for it in Italy.

- New York Style: Thin, foldable slices that became synonymous with urban dining.
- Chicago Style: Deep-dish pizza, developed in the 1940s, offering a heartier, pie-like version.
- Frozen Pizza: Introduced in the 1950s, making pizza more accessible than ever.

5. Pizza Goes Global

Today, pizza is enjoyed in virtually every corner of the globe, often adapted to reflect local tastes and ingredients. From Japan's seafood-topped pies to India's paneer-tikka pizzas, the dish has proven endlessly versatile.

The Versatility and Universal Appeal of Pizza

1. Endless Topping Possibilities

One of pizza's greatest strengths is its adaptability. Whether you prefer traditional toppings like pepperoni and mushrooms or more experimental options like truffle oil and arugula, there's a pizza for everyone.

- Vegetarian-Friendly: Loaded with vegetables and plant-based cheeses.
- Meat Lovers: Featuring sausage, bacon, and other hearty proteins.

- International Flavors: Incorporating ingredients like kimchi, curry, or smoked salmon.

2. Pizza for Every Occasion

Pizza's versatility makes it suitable for a wide range of settings, from casual gatherings to formal events.

- Casual Meals: Perfect for a quick weeknight dinner or a game-day feast.
- Special Occasions: Gourmet pizzas can be the centerpiece of a sophisticated dinner party.
- Street Food: Foldable slices or personal-sized pizzas are ideal for on-the-go dining.

3. A Comfort Food Staple

Pizza's universal appeal lies in its ability to comfort and satisfy. The combination of crispy crust, melted cheese, and flavorful toppings creates a sensory experience that's hard to resist.

Why Homemade Pizza Is the Ultimate Culinary Experience

Making pizza at home is not just about the end result—it's about the journey. The process of crafting pizza from scratch offers a sense of satisfaction and creativity that's hard to match.

1. Complete Control Over Ingredients

Homemade pizza allows you to tailor every element to your liking:

- Dough: Experiment with different types, from traditional Neapolitan to gluten-free.
- Sauce: Make your own tomato base or try unique alternatives like pesto or white sauce.
- Toppings: Use fresh, high-quality ingredients to elevate your pizza.

2. A Fun and Interactive Activity

Pizza-making is an engaging activity that brings people together:

- Family-Friendly: Kids love helping with dough rolling and topping placement.
- Pizza Nights: Hosting a make-your-own pizza night is a hit with friends.

3. The Satisfaction of Craftsmanship

There's something deeply rewarding about pulling a pizza out of the oven, knowing you created it from scratch. From kneading the dough to perfecting the bake, each step contributes to a sense of accomplishment.

4. The Joy of Experimentation

Homemade pizza encourages culinary creativity:

- Try unconventional ingredients like figs, blue cheese, or even dessert toppings.
- Experiment with cooking techniques, from wood-fired ovens to stovetop pizza pans.

Looking Ahead: A Pizza Journey

In this book, you'll discover everything you need to know to master the art of homemade pizza. From the foundations of dough-making and sauce preparation to crafting classic and innovative pies, each chapter will guide you step by step. Along the way, you'll learn tips and tricks from pizza experts, explore global flavors, and gain the confidence to experiment and innovate.

By the time you finish this book, you'll not only have a repertoire of delicious pizza recipes but also a deeper appreciation for the cultural and culinary significance of this beloved dish. Let's embark on this pizza journey together, starting with the basics and building toward becoming a true pizza artisan.

The possibilities are endless, and the satisfaction is guaranteed. Let's make pizza night a masterpiece!

Chapter 1: The Art of the Dough

Pizza dough is the foundation of every great pizza. Its texture, flavor, and structure determine whether your creation will be light and airy, chewy and satisfying, or disappointingly flat. Mastering the art of dough-making is a critical step in your pizza journey, and this chapter is dedicated to helping you understand the science, techniques, and recipes behind perfect pizza dough.

From understanding the role of each ingredient to exploring different types of dough, this chapter will empower you to create a base that complements your toppings and transforms your pizza into a masterpiece.

Understanding the Science Behind Pizza Dough

1. The Four Basic Ingredients

Every pizza dough starts with four essential ingredients: flour, water, yeast, and salt. Each plays a specific role in the dough's structure and flavor.

- Flour: The backbone of pizza dough, providing structure and elasticity.
- All-Purpose Flour: Suitable for most pizza styles.
- Bread Flour: High in protein, yielding a chewy, robust crust.
- 00 Flour: A finely milled Italian flour ideal for Neapolitan pizzas.
- Water: Hydrates the flour and activates the gluten.
- Higher hydration levels (more water) create a softer, airier crust.
- Yeast: A leavening agent that produces carbon dioxide, causing the dough to rise.
- Active Dry Yeast: Reliable and widely available.
- Instant Yeast: Convenient and fast-acting.
- Salt: Enhances flavor and strengthens gluten structure.

2. The Role of Gluten

Gluten, a protein found in wheat, is responsible for the elasticity of pizza dough. When flour is mixed with water and kneaded, gluten strands form, creating a network that traps air bubbles during fermentation. This process gives the dough its stretchiness and structure.

- High-Protein Flours: Produce more gluten, resulting in a chewier crust.

- Kneading: Develops the gluten network, ensuring the dough holds its shape.

3. Fermentation and Flavor

Fermentation occurs when yeast consumes sugars in the dough, releasing carbon dioxide and alcohol. This process not only leavens the dough but also develops complex flavors.

- Cold Fermentation: Slowing fermentation in the refrigerator enhances flavor and texture.

- Room-Temperature Fermentation: Faster but yields less nuanced flavors.

4. Hydration Levels

The hydration level of your dough (ratio of water to flour) impacts its texture and workability.

- Low Hydration (50-60%): Firm dough, suitable for thin crusts.

- Moderate Hydration (60-70%): Versatile and easy to handle.

- High Hydration (70%+): Produces airy, bubbly crusts but requires advanced handling skills.

Essential Recipes for Pizza Dough

1. Classic Pizza Dough

This versatile recipe is ideal for beginners and works for most pizza styles.

Ingredients (Makes 2 12-inch pizzas):

- 3 1/2 cups (450g) bread flour
- 1 1/4 cups (300ml) warm water
- 2 teaspoons salt
- 1 teaspoon sugar
- 2 teaspoons active dry yeast
- 2 tablespoons olive oil

Instructions:

1. Activate Yeast: Dissolve yeast and sugar in warm water. Let sit for 5-10 minutes until frothy.

2. Combine Ingredients: In a large bowl, mix flour and salt. Add yeast mixture and olive oil.

3. Knead: Knead for 8-10 minutes until smooth and elastic.

4. Proof: Place dough in a greased bowl, cover, and let rise for 1-2 hours until doubled in size.

5. Shape: Divide dough into two balls and rest for 15 minutes before shaping.

2. Whole Wheat Dough

For a nuttier flavor and added fiber, this whole wheat dough is an excellent choice.

Ingredients (Makes 2 12-inch pizzas):

- 2 cups (250g) whole wheat flour
- 1 cup (125g) bread flour
- 1 1/4 cups (300ml) warm water
- 2 teaspoons salt
- 1 teaspoon sugar
- 2 teaspoons active dry yeast
- 2 tablespoons olive oil

Instructions:

1. Mix Ingredients: Combine whole wheat and bread flour in a bowl. Add yeast mixture and olive oil.

2. Knead: Knead for 8-10 minutes until smooth and elastic.

3. Proof: Let rise for 1-2 hours until doubled in size.

3. Sourdough Pizza Dough

Sourdough offers a tangy, complex flavor and a chewy texture.

Ingredients (Makes 2 12-inch pizzas):

- 3 cups (375g) bread flour
- 1 cup (250g) sourdough starter
- 1 cup (250ml) warm water
- 2 teaspoons salt

Instructions:

1. Mix Ingredients: Combine flour, starter, water, and salt in a bowl. Mix until shaggy.

2. Knead: Knead for 8-10 minutes until smooth.

3. Cold Ferment: Refrigerate for 12-24 hours for maximum flavor.

4. Gluten-Free Dough

This gluten-free dough delivers a crisp, delicious crust without the wheat.

Ingredients (Makes 2 12-inch pizzas):

- 2 cups (240g) gluten-free all-purpose flour
- 1 teaspoon xanthan gum
- 1 teaspoon salt
- 1 teaspoon sugar
- 2 teaspoons active dry yeast
- 1 cup (250ml) warm water
- 2 tablespoons olive oil

Instructions:

1. Mix Dry Ingredients: Combine flour, xanthan gum, salt, and sugar in a bowl.

2. Activate Yeast: Dissolve yeast in warm water and let sit for 5 minutes.

3. Combine: Add yeast mixture and olive oil to dry ingredients. Mix until smooth.

4. Proof: Cover and let rise for 1 hour.

Tips for Kneading, Proofing, and Texture

1. Kneading Techniques

Proper kneading develops the gluten network, ensuring elasticity and structure.

- Hand Kneading: Use the heel of your hand to stretch and fold the dough.
- Stand Mixer: Use a dough hook for convenience. Knead for 5-7 minutes on medium speed.

2. Proofing for Perfect Rise

Proofing allows the dough to rise, creating air pockets that result in a light, airy crust.

- Room-Temperature Proofing: Ideal for quick results, typically 1-2 hours.
- Cold Proofing: Refrigerate for 24-48 hours to enhance flavor and texture.

3. Achieving the Perfect Texture

- Soft and Elastic: Use moderate hydration and thorough kneading.
- Crispy and Thin: Roll dough thin and use low hydration.
- Chewy and Airy: Opt for high hydration and long fermentation.

Common Dough-Making Challenges and Solutions

- Sticky Dough: Add small amounts of flour during kneading but avoid over-flouring.
- Dense Crust: Ensure proper kneading and proofing to incorporate enough air.
- Tough Dough: Avoid over-kneading and use the right flour type.

Conclusion: Mastering the Art of Dough

The dough is the heart and soul of every pizza, and mastering it opens the door to endless culinary possibilities. By understanding the science behind the ingredients, experimenting with different recipes, and perfecting your techniques, you can create pizza dough that elevates your homemade pies to new heights.

In the next chapter, we'll explore the tools and equipment needed to take your pizza-making skills to the next level. From pizza stones to high-heat ovens, you'll learn how to create the ideal environment for baking your perfect crust. Let's keep building the foundation for your pizza mastery!

Chapter 2: Essential Tools for Pizza Making

Making pizza at home is an art, and having the right tools can transform your kitchen into a professional pizza-making station. While crafting the perfect dough and assembling flavorful toppings are crucial, the equipment you use plays a significant role in achieving restaurant-quality results. This chapter will guide you through the must-have tools for pizza making, explain the benefits of high-heat cooking methods, and provide tips for setting up your ideal home pizza-making station.

Why Tools Matter

The success of homemade pizza often hinges on the tools you use. A well-equipped kitchen ensures your pizza cooks evenly, achieves the right texture, and captures the authentic flavors of traditional pies. From creating the perfect crust to managing high temperatures, the right equipment simplifies the process and elevates your results.

1. Precision and Consistency

Specialized tools like pizza stones and peels provide the consistency needed to replicate professional techniques at home.

2. Enhancing Flavor and Texture

Equipment like high-heat ovens and pizza steels helps achieve the ideal balance of a crispy crust and perfectly cooked toppings.

3. Efficiency and Convenience

With the right tools, you can streamline the pizza-making process, saving time while improving results.

Must-Have Equipment for Pizza Making

1. Pizza Stones

A pizza stone is one of the most essential tools for any pizza enthusiast. Made from ceramic or cordierite, pizza stones mimic the high heat of a professional oven, ensuring a crispy, evenly baked crust.

- How It Works: The stone absorbs and retains heat, distributing it evenly to the dough.
- Benefits:
- Creates a crispy, golden crust.
- Prevents soggy bottoms by absorbing excess moisture.
- Versatile for baking bread and pastries.

Tips for Use:

- Preheat the stone in your oven for at least 30 minutes before baking.
- Place the dough directly on the hot stone for best results.
- Avoid washing with soap; clean with water and a scrubber to maintain its porous surface.

2. Pizza Steel

Pizza steel is a game-changer for home pizza makers, especially those seeking the perfect Neapolitan-style crust. Made from high-grade steel, it conducts heat even better than a stone.

- How It Works: The steel retains and transfers intense heat, cooking the pizza quickly and evenly.
- Benefits:
- Produces a crisp, charred crust similar to a wood-fired oven.
- Heats up faster and retains heat longer than a pizza stone.
- Durable and easy to maintain.

Tips for Use:

- Preheat in the oven for 30-45 minutes.
- Allow the steel to cool completely before cleaning to avoid warping.

3. Pizza Peel

A pizza peel is essential for transferring your pizza to and from the oven without damaging the crust or toppings. Peels come in various materials, each with unique benefits.

- Types of Peels:
- Wooden Peels: Ideal for launching pizzas into the oven.
- Metal Peels: Better for retrieving pizzas once cooked.

Tips for Use:

- Dust the peel with flour or cornmeal to prevent sticking.
- Practice sliding the pizza onto the peel to perfect your technique.
- Keep the peel surface dry and clean for smoother transfers.

4. Ovens

The oven is the cornerstone of pizza making. While not everyone has access to a wood-fired oven, there are several home-friendly options to achieve high-quality results.

- Home Ovens:
- Preheat to the maximum temperature (usually 500°F or higher).
- Use a pizza stone or steel for better heat distribution.
- Pizza Ovens:
- Countertop pizza ovens or outdoor wood-fired ovens are ideal for achieving temperatures of 800°F or more.
- Brands like Ooni and Roccbox offer portable, high-heat options for home use.
- Alternative Methods:
- Cast iron pans or grill setups can replicate high-heat environments.

5. Rolling Pins

While many pizza styles benefit from hand-stretching, a rolling pin is useful for achieving thin, uniform crusts.

- Types:
- Classic Wooden Rolling Pin: Versatile and easy to handle.
- French Rolling Pin: Tapered ends for more precise control.

6. Dough Scrapers

A dough scraper is a versatile tool for dividing and shaping dough, ensuring smooth and consistent results.

- Uses:
- Dividing dough into portions.
- Scraping dough from countertops.
- Shaping and folding during proofing.

7. Thermometers

A good thermometer ensures precision, whether you're checking dough temperature or oven heat.

- Types:
- Instant-Read Thermometers: Perfect for measuring water or dough temperatures.
- Infrared Thermometers: Ideal for gauging the temperature of pizza stones or steels.

8. Pizza Cutter or Rocker Blade

A high-quality pizza cutter ensures clean, even slices without dragging toppings.

- Types:
- Wheel Cutters: Easy to use for standard slicing.
- Rocker Blades: Ideal for larger pizzas or precise cuts.

The Benefits of High-Heat Cooking Methods

High-heat cooking is essential for achieving the perfect pizza crust and ensuring toppings cook evenly without overbaking the dough.

1. Crisp Crusts

High heat allows the outer layer of the dough to crisp up quickly while retaining a soft, airy interior.

2. Fast Cooking Times

Professional ovens reach temperatures of 800°F or more, cooking pizzas in under two minutes. Replicating this at home requires maximizing your oven's heat.

3. Enhanced Flavor

Quick cooking caramelizes the dough's sugars and toppings, creating a smoky, complex flavor profile.

Tips for High-Heat Cooking at Home

- Preheat Thoroughly: Allow your oven, stone, or steel to reach maximum temperature before cooking.
- Positioning: Place the stone or steel on the top rack for better browning.
- Monitor Closely: High heat requires attention to avoid overcooking.

Setting Up a Home Pizza-Making Station

Creating a dedicated pizza-making station enhances your workflow and ensures consistent results.

1. Choose Your Space

Designate a counter or table with ample room for rolling, topping, and staging your pizzas.

2. Organize Your Tools

Keep your essential tools within reach:

- Pizza peel, stone, or steel.
- Dough scraper and rolling pin.
- Toppings and sauces.

3. Prep Ingredients in Advance

- Portion toppings into bowls for easy access.
- Keep cheeses grated and sauces prepared.

4. Set Up a Cooling and Serving Area

- Use racks for cooling hot pizzas.
- Keep a large cutting board ready for slicing and serving.

Common Mistakes and How to Avoid Them

- Uneven Cooking: Rotate the pizza midway through baking for even heat distribution.
- Soggy Crusts: Avoid overloading with sauce or toppings.
- Sticking to the Peel: Use enough flour or cornmeal to ensure smooth transfers.

Conclusion: Equipping Yourself for Success

With the right tools and setup, your home kitchen can rival the best pizzerias. From mastering the art of transferring pizzas with a peel to using high-heat equipment for perfectly crisp crusts, the tools outlined in this chapter are your foundation for pizza-making excellence.

In the next chapter, we'll dive into perfecting the sauce—an essential component that ties your pizza together. From classic tomato bases to innovative alternatives, you'll learn how to craft the perfect sauce for any style of pizza. Let's continue this delicious journey!

Chapter 3: Perfecting the Sauce

The sauce is the heart of any great pizza. While the dough provides the structure and the toppings add flair, the sauce binds it all together, delivering flavor and depth to every bite. A well-made pizza sauce enhances the overall experience, complementing the crust, cheese, and toppings without overpowering them.

In this chapter, we'll explore how to craft the perfect pizza sauce, from the classic tomato base to creative alternatives like white sauce, pesto, and barbecue sauce. You'll learn how to balance flavors—acidity, sweetness, and seasoning—to create sauces that elevate your homemade pizzas to new heights.

The Role of Sauce in Pizza Making

The sauce serves as the foundation for the pizza's flavor profile. A great sauce can enhance the natural sweetness of tomatoes, add a touch of tangy brightness, or provide a creamy contrast to bold toppings.

Why Sauce Matters

1. Flavor Anchor: It ties together the diverse elements of the pizza.
2. Moisture Balance: Provides moisture without making the crust soggy.
3. Versatility: Offers endless opportunities for experimentation and creativity.

Classic Tomato Sauce: Simple and Flavorful

A classic tomato sauce is the most widely used base for pizza. Its simplicity allows the other components to shine, making it the perfect choice for a traditional Margherita or New York-style pizza.

Ingredients for Classic Tomato Sauce

- Tomatoes: The cornerstone of a great sauce.
    - San Marzano Tomatoes: Known for their sweetness and low acidity, these Italian tomatoes are the gold standard for pizza sauce.
    - Alternative Options: Roma tomatoes or high-quality canned tomatoes.
    - Olive Oil: Adds richness and enhances flavor.
    - Garlic: Provides depth and a touch of savoriness.
    - Salt: Enhances natural flavors.
    - Fresh Basil: Adds an aromatic, herbaceous note.
    - Optional Sweetener: A pinch of sugar balances acidity if the tomatoes are too tart.

Recipe: Classic Tomato Sauce

Ingredients:

- 1 can (28 ounces) San Marzano tomatoes
- 2 tablespoons olive oil
- 2 garlic cloves, minced
- 1 teaspoon salt
- 1/2 teaspoon black pepper
- 1/2 teaspoon sugar (optional)
- 4-5 fresh basil leaves, torn

Instructions:

1. Prepare the Tomatoes: Crush the tomatoes by hand or use an immersion blender for a smoother texture.
2. Cook the Garlic: Heat olive oil in a saucepan over medium heat. Sauté garlic until fragrant but not browned.
3. Simmer the Sauce: Add the tomatoes, salt, pepper, and sugar (if using). Simmer for 20-30 minutes, stirring occasionally.
4. Finish with Basil: Add fresh basil leaves during the last few minutes of cooking.

Pro Tip: For a no-cook version, blend the ingredients and let the flavors meld for an hour before spreading on the dough.

Creative Alternatives to Tomato Sauce

For those looking to experiment, alternative sauces can transform the flavor profile of your pizza. Here are some popular options:

1. White Sauce (Béchamel)

A creamy, rich white sauce is perfect for pairing with delicate toppings like mushrooms, spinach, or seafood.

Ingredients:

- 2 tablespoons butter
- 2 tablespoons all-purpose flour
- 1 cup whole milk
- 1/4 teaspoon nutmeg
- Salt and pepper to taste

Instructions:

1. Make a Roux: Melt butter in a saucepan over medium heat. Add flour and whisk until smooth.
2. Add Milk: Gradually pour in milk, whisking continuously to avoid lumps.
3. Season: Add nutmeg, salt, and pepper. Cook until thickened, about 5 minutes.

Pro Tip: Add Parmesan cheese for extra flavor.

2. Pesto Sauce

Pesto is a vibrant, herbaceous sauce that pairs beautifully with mozzarella, tomatoes, and roasted vegetables.

Ingredients:

- 2 cups fresh basil leaves
- 1/4 cup pine nuts
- 1/4 cup Parmesan cheese, grated
- 2 garlic cloves
- 1/2 cup olive oil
- Salt to taste

Instructions:

1. Blend Ingredients: Combine basil, pine nuts, Parmesan, and garlic in a food processor. Blend while slowly adding olive oil.

2. Season: Add salt to taste.

Pro Tip: Use arugula, spinach, or kale as a base for alternative pesto variations.

3. Barbecue Sauce

A smoky, tangy barbecue sauce adds a bold twist to pizzas topped with chicken, bacon, or red onions.

Ingredients:

- 1 cup ketchup
- 1/4 cup apple cider vinegar
- 2 tablespoons brown sugar
- 1 tablespoon Worcestershire sauce
- 1 teaspoon smoked paprika

Instructions:

1. Combine Ingredients: Mix all ingredients in a saucepan.

2. Simmer: Cook over low heat for 10-15 minutes until thickened.

Pro Tip: Adjust sweetness and smokiness by varying the sugar and paprika levels.

4. Olive Tapenade

This briny, bold sauce is ideal for Mediterranean-inspired pizzas with toppings like feta, artichokes, and sun-dried tomatoes.

Ingredients:

- 1 cup pitted olives (Kalamata or green)
- 2 tablespoons capers
- 2 tablespoons olive oil
- 1 garlic clove
- Lemon juice to taste

Instructions:

1. Blend Ingredients: Combine olives, capers, olive oil, and garlic in a food processor. Blend to a coarse paste.

2. Adjust Flavor: Add lemon juice to brighten the flavor.

Balancing Acidity, Sweetness, and Seasoning

Crafting the perfect pizza sauce requires a careful balance of flavors. Here's how to adjust your sauce to achieve harmony:

1. Managing Acidity

- Too Acidic: Add a pinch of sugar or a splash of cream to mellow the sharpness.
- Too Bland: Incorporate a touch of vinegar or lemon juice to brighten flavors.

2. Enhancing Sweetness

- Use naturally sweet ingredients like roasted garlic, caramelized onions, or fresh basil.
- Avoid over-sweetening, which can overpower the sauce.

3. Seasoning Wisely

- Salt is crucial for enhancing flavors but should not dominate the sauce.
- Incorporate spices like oregano, thyme, or red pepper flakes for complexity.

Tips for Perfecting Your Sauce

1. Use High-Quality Ingredients

- Fresh tomatoes, aromatic garlic, and good olive oil make all the difference.

2. Avoid Overcooking

- Overcooking can dull flavors and make the sauce too thick.

3. Adjust Consistency

- Blend or strain the sauce for a smoother texture.
- Reduce the sauce over low heat for a thicker, more concentrated flavor.

4. Pair Sauce with Pizza Style

- Match rich, creamy sauces with delicate toppings.

- Pair bold, tangy sauces with hearty meats and vegetables.

Creative Variations for Experimentation

- Spicy Arrabbiata Sauce: Add crushed red pepper flakes to your tomato sauce for heat.
- Garlic Herb Oil: Brush dough with a mix of olive oil, minced garlic, and fresh herbs for a light, flavorful base.
- Hummus Spread: Use hummus as a base for Middle Eastern-inspired pizzas.

Conclusion: The Power of Sauce

The sauce is more than just a layer between the crust and toppings—it's the foundation of your pizza's flavor. By mastering classic tomato sauces and experimenting with creative alternatives, you can tailor each pizza to your unique tastes and preferences. Whether you're crafting a traditional Margherita or a bold barbecue chicken pie, the right sauce will elevate your creation.

In the next chapter, we'll dive into cheese selection, exploring how different types of cheese contribute to flavor, texture, and visual appeal. Let's keep building toward your perfect homemade pizza!

Chapter 4: Exploring Cheese Options

Cheese is the crown jewel of pizza, melting into a gooey, golden layer that ties together the crust, sauce, and toppings. It adds flavor, texture, and a satisfying richness that makes pizza irresistible. While mozzarella reigns supreme in the pizza world, the diversity of cheese options—both dairy and non-dairy—offers limitless possibilities for creating unique and delicious pies.

In this chapter, we'll delve into the best cheeses for pizza, including classic choices like mozzarella and Parmesan, explore non-dairy cheese alternatives for vegan pizzas, and provide tips for layering and blending cheeses to achieve the perfect balance of flavor and texture.

The Best Cheeses for Melting and Flavor

Not all cheeses are created equal when it comes to pizza. The ideal cheese should melt smoothly, stretch beautifully, and complement the other ingredients. Here's a closer look at some of the best cheeses for pizza:

1. Mozzarella: The Gold Standard

Mozzarella is the most popular cheese for pizza, thanks to its excellent melting qualities and mild, creamy flavor.

Types of Mozzarella:

1. Fresh Mozzarella:

- Packed in water, fresh mozzarella has a soft texture and a slightly tangy flavor.
- Best for Neapolitan-style pizzas.
- Requires draining and patting dry to avoid excess moisture.

2. Low-Moisture Mozzarella:

- Firmer and saltier than fresh mozzarella.
- Melts evenly and browns beautifully, making it ideal for New York-style pizzas.

3. Buffalo Mozzarella:

- Made from buffalo milk, it has a richer flavor and creamier texture.
- Best used for authentic Italian pizzas.

2. Parmesan: A Flavor Booster

Parmesan is a hard, aged cheese with a nutty, salty flavor that enhances the overall taste of pizza.

- How to Use:
- Grate Parmesan over the pizza after baking for a savory kick.
- Blend with mozzarella for added depth in the cheese layer.
- Pro Tip: Choose high-quality, aged Parmesan (Parmigiano-Reggiano) for the best flavor.

3. Provolone: A Creamy Complement

Provolone is a semi-hard cheese with a slightly tangy flavor. It pairs well with mozzarella, adding richness and complexity.

- How to Use:
- Blend with mozzarella for a creamier texture.
- Use sharp provolone for a more pronounced flavor.

4. Cheddar: A Bold Option

Cheddar brings sharpness and a distinct flavor to pizzas, particularly those with barbecue or meat toppings.

- How to Use:
- Combine with mozzarella to balance its low melting point.
- Best for non-traditional pizzas like barbecue chicken or cheeseburger-inspired pies.

5. Ricotta: Creamy and Versatile

Ricotta is a fresh cheese with a smooth, creamy texture and mild flavor, perfect for adding richness to pizza.

- How to Use:
- Dollop onto the pizza in small amounts.
- Mix with herbs or garlic for added flavor.

6. Gouda: A Smoky Twist

Gouda is a semi-hard cheese with a creamy texture and a mild, smoky flavor.

- How to Use:
- Pair with barbecue sauce or smoked meats.
- Use aged Gouda for a nuttier flavor.

7. Fontina: A Melting Marvel

Fontina is a semi-soft cheese known for its excellent melting properties and buttery flavor.

- How to Use:
- Combine with mozzarella for a rich, stretchy layer.
- Ideal for white pizzas and gourmet toppings.

8. Blue Cheese: A Bold Statement

Blue cheese adds a tangy, sharp flavor that pairs well with sweet or savory ingredients.

- How to Use:
- Crumble over pizzas with figs, honey, or caramelized onions.
- Use sparingly to avoid overpowering the other flavors.

9. Goat Cheese: Tangy and Creamy

Goat cheese has a distinctive tanginess and creamy texture, making it a popular choice for artisan pizzas.

- How to Use:
- Crumble over pizzas with roasted vegetables or fruit.
- Mix with herbs for added flavor.

Non-Dairy Cheese Alternatives for Vegan Pizzas

As plant-based diets grow in popularity, non-dairy cheese alternatives have become more accessible and versatile. Modern vegan cheeses offer excellent melting properties and bold flavors, making them a viable option for vegan pizzas.

1. Types of Non-Dairy Cheeses

1.1. Cashew-Based Cheeses

- Made from blended cashews, these cheeses have a creamy texture and nutty flavor.

- Best for creamy white sauces or dolloping.

1.2. Almond-Based Cheeses

- Similar to cashew-based options but with a slightly firmer texture.

- Ideal for grating or slicing.

1.3. Coconut Oil-Based Cheeses

- Mimics the melt and stretch of mozzarella.

- Brands like Violife and Miyoko's are popular for their authentic flavor.

1.4. Soy-Based Cheeses

- Affordable and widely available.

- Brands like Daiya offer soy-based mozzarella and cheddar shreds.

1.5. Nutritional Yeast

- A savory, cheesy-flavored seasoning that can be sprinkled on pizzas.

- Often combined with cashew or almond-based sauces.

2. DIY Vegan Cheese Recipes

2.1. Vegan Mozzarella

- Ingredients: Cashews, tapioca starch, lemon juice, garlic, salt, water.

- Instructions: Blend all ingredients until smooth, heat in a saucepan, and stir until thickened.

2.2. Creamy Vegan Ricotta

- Ingredients: Almonds, lemon juice, olive oil, garlic, salt.

- Instructions: Blend ingredients until smooth and use as a topping or sauce.

Tips for Layering and Blending Cheeses

1. Start with a Base Layer

- Use mozzarella or a mild cheese as the foundation to ensure even melting and coverage.

2. Add Flavor Boosters

- Sprinkle aged cheeses like Parmesan or Pecorino on top for extra flavor.

3. Balance Textures

- Combine creamy cheeses (ricotta, goat cheese) with firmer ones (fontina, provolone) for contrast.

4. Avoid Overloading

- Too much cheese can weigh down the crust and prevent even cooking.

5. Experiment with Ratios

- Mix cheeses in different proportions to find your ideal balance of melt, flavor, and texture.

Pairing Cheeses with Toppings

1. Classic Margherita

- Fresh mozzarella with a sprinkle of Parmesan.

2. Barbecue Chicken

- Mozzarella, cheddar, and Gouda for smoky richness.

3. Veggie Lovers

- Fontina, goat cheese, or ricotta with roasted vegetables.

4. Sweet and Savory

- Blue cheese with figs or honey for a gourmet twist.

Conclusion: The Cheese Factor

Cheese is the soul of pizza, bringing flavor, texture, and visual appeal to every slice. From the stretch of fresh mozzarella to the tang of goat cheese or the smoky richness of Gouda, the right cheese can elevate your pizza to new heights. Whether you're sticking with classics or experimenting with non-dairy alternatives, the possibilities are endless.

In the next chapter, we'll explore how to create the perfect harmony of toppings, ensuring that every bite is a flavorful masterpiece. Let's continue crafting the ultimate homemade pizza!

Chapter 5: Traditional Italian Pizzas

When you think of pizza, you might envision gooey cheese, perfectly crisp crusts, and vibrant toppings, but the roots of pizza lie in its simplest and most traditional forms. Italian pizzas, particularly those born in Naples, showcase the essence of simplicity and balance. With just a few high-quality ingredients and careful techniques, traditional Italian pizzas like Margherita, Marinara, and Quattro Formaggi have captivated palates worldwide for centuries.

This chapter will guide you through the art of crafting these iconic pizzas, explore the techniques behind authentic Neapolitan pizza-making, and emphasize the importance of using the best ingredients to achieve genuine Italian flavors.

The Legacy of Traditional Italian Pizzas

The Origin of Italian Pizzas

The origins of pizza can be traced back to Naples, Italy, where flatbreads were topped with simple, local ingredients. Initially, pizza was food for the working class, affordable and portable. Over time, it evolved into an art form, with distinct styles emerging based on regional preferences.

What Makes Italian Pizzas Unique?

1. Minimalism: Italian pizzas rely on a few high-quality ingredients, allowing each component to shine.
2. Authenticity: Traditional recipes are rooted in centuries-old techniques.
3. Focus on Freshness: Seasonal, local ingredients are prioritized for maximum flavor.
4. Cultural Identity: Pizza is more than food in Italy; it's a tradition, a craft, and a source of pride.

The Importance of High-Quality Ingredients

Italian pizzas thrive on simplicity, which means every ingredient matters. Here's why quality is non-negotiable:

1. Flour

- 00 Flour: Finely milled, soft wheat flour with low protein content, ideal for creating elastic, airy dough.

- Why It Matters: Produces a light, tender crust with a crisp exterior.

2. Tomatoes

- San Marzano Tomatoes: Grown in Italy's volcanic soil, these tomatoes are sweet, low in acidity, and rich in flavor.

- Why It Matters: The foundation of a balanced, vibrant sauce.

3. Cheese

- Fresh Mozzarella di Bufala: Creamy, tangy buffalo milk mozzarella is the gold standard for Italian pizzas.

- Parmesan and Pecorino: Add sharpness and depth.

4. Olive Oil

- Extra-Virgin Olive Oil: A drizzle adds richness and enhances flavors.

5. Fresh Herbs

- Basil and Oregano: Essential for classic Italian flavor.

Techniques for Authentic Neapolitan Pizza

Neapolitan pizza, recognized by UNESCO as part of the world's cultural heritage, is defined by its thin, soft crust and vibrant toppings. Here's how to replicate it:

1. The Dough

Neapolitan pizza dough is simple, with just four ingredients: flour, water, yeast, and salt. The key is the technique.

- Hydration Level: Aim for a 65-70% hydration level for a light, airy crust.

- Kneading: Knead until smooth and elastic.

- Fermentation: Allow for slow, cold fermentation (12-24 hours) to develop flavor.

2. The Shaping

- Hand-stretch the dough to preserve air pockets, ensuring a soft, pillowy texture.

- Aim for a thin center with a slightly raised edge (cornicione).

3. The Oven

- Authentic Neapolitan pizzas are cooked in wood-fired ovens at 800-900°F, baking in under 90 seconds.

- At Home: Use a pizza stone or steel in the hottest oven setting to mimic these conditions.

Recipes for Traditional Italian Pizzas

1. Pizza Margherita

The quintessential Italian pizza, Margherita is a masterpiece of simplicity, showcasing the colors of the Italian flag: red (tomato), white (mozzarella), and green (basil).

Ingredients (Serves 2):

- 2 Neapolitan pizza dough balls
- 1 cup San Marzano tomato sauce
- 8 ounces fresh mozzarella, sliced
- Fresh basil leaves
- Extra-virgin olive oil
- Salt to taste

Instructions:

1. Preheat the Oven: Heat a pizza stone in the oven at 500°F (or highest setting) for 45 minutes.

2. Prepare the Dough: Stretch each dough ball into a 10-12 inch circle.

3. Add the Sauce: Spread a thin layer of tomato sauce on the dough, leaving a 1-inch border.

4. Layer the Cheese: Scatter mozzarella slices evenly.

5. Bake: Transfer the pizza to the hot stone and bake for 5-7 minutes, until the crust is golden and the cheese is bubbling.

6. Finish: Add fresh basil leaves and drizzle with olive oil.

Pro Tip: Serve immediately to enjoy the mozzarella's creamy texture.

2. Pizza Marinara

Pizza Marinara is a tomato-forward pizza without cheese, highlighting the bold flavors of garlic and oregano.

Ingredients (Serves 2):

- 2 Neapolitan pizza dough balls
- 1 cup San Marzano tomato sauce
- 2 garlic cloves, thinly sliced
- 1 teaspoon dried oregano
- Extra-virgin olive oil
- Salt to taste

Instructions:

1. Preheat the Oven: Heat a pizza stone to 500°F.
2. Prepare the Dough: Stretch each dough ball into a 10-12 inch circle.
3. Add the Sauce: Spread a thin layer of tomato sauce on the dough.
4. Top with Garlic and Oregano: Distribute sliced garlic and sprinkle oregano evenly.
5. Bake: Transfer to the hot stone and bake for 5-7 minutes.
6. Finish: Drizzle with olive oil before serving.

Pro Tip: Use fresh oregano for a more aromatic flavor.

3. Pizza Quattro Formaggi

The "four cheese" pizza is a rich, indulgent treat, blending different cheeses for a harmonious balance of flavors.

Ingredients (Serves 2):

- 2 Neapolitan pizza dough balls
- 1/2 cup tomato sauce (optional)
- 4 ounces mozzarella, shredded
- 2 ounces Gorgonzola cheese
- 2 ounces Parmesan, grated
- 2 ounces Fontina, diced
- Extra-virgin olive oil

Instructions:

1. Preheat the Oven: Heat a pizza stone to 500°F.
2. Prepare the Dough: Stretch each dough ball into a 10-12 inch circle.

3. Add the Base: Spread tomato sauce if desired, or leave the dough bare.

4. Layer the Cheeses: Evenly distribute mozzarella, Gorgonzola, Parmesan, and Fontina.

5. Bake: Cook for 5-7 minutes until the cheese is melted and bubbly.

6. Finish: Drizzle with olive oil before serving.

Pro Tip: Serve with a light salad to balance the richness of the cheeses.

Tips for Perfecting Traditional Italian Pizzas

1. Choose the Best Ingredients

High-quality ingredients are the cornerstone of Italian pizzas. Invest in authentic products like San Marzano tomatoes, fresh mozzarella, and good olive oil.

2. Master the Dough

- Practice kneading and shaping techniques to achieve an elastic, airy dough.

- Experiment with fermentation times to enhance flavor.

3. Embrace Simplicity

Less is more with traditional Italian pizzas. Avoid overloading with toppings to let the flavors shine.

4. Cook at High Heat

Replicate the intense heat of a wood-fired oven by preheating a pizza stone or steel.

Conclusion: Celebrating Italian Tradition

Traditional Italian pizzas like Margherita, Marinara, and Quattro Formaggi are timeless classics that embody the essence of simplicity and balance. By mastering authentic techniques, using high-quality ingredients, and embracing the Italian philosophy of minimalism, you can create pizzas that honor their rich heritage.

In the next chapter, we'll explore American classics, including New York-style and Chicago deep-dish pizzas, diving into the techniques and flavors that have made these styles iconic in their own right. Let's continue the journey of pizza mastery!

Chapter 6: American Classics

American pizza has carved its own identity in the culinary world, offering unique variations that reflect regional flavors and preferences. From the foldable, crispy New York slice to the indulgent layers of Chicago deep-dish and the caramelized edges of Detroit square pizza, these styles showcase the diversity of pizza in the United States.

In this chapter, we'll explore the history, characteristics, and techniques behind three iconic American pizza styles. You'll also learn recipes and tips for recreating their authentic textures and flavors in your home kitchen.

The Evolution of American Pizza

Pizza arrived in the United States with Italian immigrants in the late 19th and early 20th centuries. Initially concentrated in cities like New York and Chicago, pizza evolved to suit local tastes and ingredients. Over time, different regions developed their own styles, each with unique characteristics.

What Defines American Pizza?

1. Generosity: American pizzas often feature larger sizes, more toppings, and thicker layers of cheese compared to their Italian counterparts.

2. Diversity: Each region puts its own spin on pizza, from crust styles to sauce variations.

3. Creativity: Innovative toppings and combinations reflect the melting pot of American cuisine.

1. New York-Style Pizza

History and Characteristics

New York-style pizza is perhaps the most iconic of American pizzas. Its origins trace back to Italian immigrants in the early 20th century, who adapted traditional Neapolitan recipes to local ingredients and preferences. The result is a thin, foldable slice with a crisp yet chewy crust.

Key Features:
- Thin Crust: Crisp along the edges but soft enough to fold.
- Light Sauce: Tomato-forward with a touch of herbs and sweetness.
- Generous Cheese: A blanket of low-moisture mozzarella.

Recipe: New York-Style Pizza

Ingredients (Serves 4):

For the Dough:
- 4 cups bread flour
- 1 1/2 cups water, warm
- 1 teaspoon sugar
- 1 teaspoon salt
- 1 teaspoon active dry yeast
- 2 tablespoons olive oil

For the Sauce:
- 1 can (28 ounces) San Marzano tomatoes
- 2 tablespoons olive oil
- 1 teaspoon oregano
- 1 teaspoon sugar
- 1/2 teaspoon salt

For the Toppings:
- 16 ounces low-moisture mozzarella, shredded
- Optional: Pepperoni, mushrooms, or sausage

Instructions:

1. Make the Dough:
- Dissolve yeast and sugar in warm water. Let sit for 5 minutes.
- Combine flour and salt in a bowl. Add yeast mixture and olive oil.
- Knead until smooth and elastic (8-10 minutes).
- Let the dough rise for 1-2 hours or until doubled in size.

2. Prepare the Sauce:
- Blend the tomatoes with olive oil, oregano, sugar, and salt.
- Simmer for 15 minutes to thicken slightly.

3. Preheat the Oven:
- Heat a pizza stone or steel at 500°F for at least 30 minutes.

4. Assemble the Pizza:

- Roll out the dough into a 14-inch circle.
- Spread a thin layer of sauce, leaving a 1-inch border.
- Sprinkle mozzarella evenly. Add toppings if desired.

5. Bake:

- Transfer to the hot stone and bake for 7-9 minutes until the crust is golden and the cheese is bubbling.

Pro Tip: Serve slices with a sprinkle of Parmesan and red pepper flakes for an authentic touch.

2. Chicago Deep-Dish Pizza

History and Characteristics

Invented in the 1940s at Pizzeria Uno, Chicago deep-dish pizza is a hearty, indulgent creation. Unlike most pizzas, the crust forms a tall edge, creating a "pie" filled with layers of cheese, toppings, and chunky tomato sauce.

Key Features:

- Thick Crust: Buttery and flaky, resembling a pie crust.
- Cheese First: Layers of cheese and toppings are added before the sauce.
- Chunky Tomato Sauce: A rich, flavorful topping layer.

Recipe: Chicago Deep-Dish Pizza

Ingredients (Serves 4):

For the Dough:

- 3 1/4 cups all-purpose flour
- 1/2 cup cornmeal
- 1 teaspoon salt
- 1 teaspoon sugar
- 2 1/4 teaspoons active dry yeast
- 1 cup warm water

- 1/3 cup butter, melted

For the Sauce:

- 1 can (28 ounces) crushed tomatoes
- 2 tablespoons olive oil
- 1 garlic clove, minced
- 1 teaspoon oregano
- 1 teaspoon sugar
- 1/2 teaspoon salt

For the Filling:

- 16 ounces mozzarella, sliced
- 1/2 pound Italian sausage, cooked
- Optional: Green peppers, mushrooms, onions

Instructions:

1. Make the Dough:

- Combine flour, cornmeal, salt, sugar, and yeast.
- Add warm water and melted butter. Knead until smooth.
- Let rise for 1 hour.

2. Prepare the Sauce:

- Sauté garlic in olive oil. Add crushed tomatoes, oregano, sugar, and salt. Simmer for 20 minutes.

3. Preheat the Oven:

- Heat oven to 425°F.

4. Assemble the Pizza:

- Roll out the dough and press it into a greased deep-dish pan, covering the sides.
- Layer mozzarella slices at the bottom. Add sausage and other toppings.
- Pour tomato sauce over the top.

5. Bake:

- Bake for 25-30 minutes until the crust is golden. Let cool for 5 minutes before slicing.

Pro Tip: Use a springform pan for easier slicing and serving.

3. Detroit Square Pizza

History and Characteristics

Detroit-style pizza originated in the 1940s at Buddy's Rendezvous. Baked in rectangular steel pans, it features a thick, airy crust with crispy, caramelized edges from cheese melted along the sides.

Key Features:

- Rectangular Shape: Baked in steel pans originally used for auto parts.
- Caramelized Crust: Cheese melts into the edges, creating crispy corners.
- Toppings Over Sauce: Sauce is drizzled on top after baking.

Recipe: Detroit Square Pizza

Ingredients (Serves 4):

For the Dough:

- 4 cups bread flour
- 1 teaspoon salt
- 1 teaspoon sugar
- 1 teaspoon yeast
- 1 1/4 cups warm water
- 2 tablespoons olive oil

For the Toppings:

- 16 ounces Wisconsin brick cheese (or mozzarella), shredded
- 1 cup tomato sauce
- Optional: Pepperoni, sausage, or vegetables

Instructions:

1. Make the Dough:

- Combine flour, salt, sugar, and yeast. Add warm water and olive oil. Mix until smooth.
- Let rise for 2 hours.

2. Preheat the Oven:

- Heat oven to 500°F.

3. Prepare the Pan:

- Grease a rectangular steel pan with olive oil. Spread dough evenly, pushing into the corners.

4. Add Cheese and Toppings:

- Sprinkle cheese to cover the dough completely, ensuring some touches the edges. Add toppings if desired.

5. Bake:

- Bake for 12-15 minutes until the edges are crispy and golden.

6. Add Sauce:

- Drizzle tomato sauce in lines across the top.

Pro Tip: Let the pizza cool for a few minutes to allow the cheese to set before cutting.

Regional Variations and Unique Characteristics

While New York, Chicago, and Detroit pizzas are iconic, other regions have developed their own styles:

- St. Louis Pizza: Thin, cracker-like crust with Provel cheese.
- California Pizza: Focuses on fresh, innovative toppings like arugula, goat cheese, and figs.
- New Haven Pizza (Apizza): Thin, charred crust with minimal cheese.

Tips for Authentic Textures and Flavors

1. Invest in Quality Ingredients: Use the best flour, cheese, and tomatoes you can find.
2. Preheat Your Oven: High heat is essential for replicating pizzeria results.
3. Experiment with Dough Hydration: Adjust water levels for different crust styles.
4. Use the Right Pan: Detroit and Chicago pizzas rely on specific pans for their texture.

Conclusion: Celebrating American Pizza Diversity

American pizza styles celebrate creativity and regional pride, offering something for every taste. Whether it's the foldable slices of New York, the indulgent layers of Chicago, or the crispy edges of Detroit, each style tells a unique story. By mastering these classics, you'll not only honor their rich history but also expand your pizza repertoire.

In the next chapter, we'll explore flatbreads and thin crusts, diving into recipes and techniques for light, crispy pizzas perfect for any occasion. Let's continue crafting pizza perfection!

Chapter 7: Flatbreads and Thin Crusts

Flatbreads and thin-crust pizzas represent the lighter, crisper side of pizza-making, offering a delicate base that lets toppings shine. These styles are perfect for those who appreciate balance and simplicity, where the crust is more of a canvas than the centerpiece. Roman-style pizzas, cracker-thin crusts, and lavash-based creations are versatile, quick to prepare, and endlessly adaptable.

This chapter will explore the techniques and recipes needed to master ultra-thin, crispy crusts and offer ideas for pairing them with light, fresh toppings.

The Appeal of Flatbreads and Thin Crusts

Thin-crust pizzas and flatbreads are ideal for showcasing high-quality toppings without overwhelming the palate. Here's why they've gained popularity:

- Crisp Texture: A satisfying crunch that contrasts beautifully with soft toppings.

- Balanced Bites: Each bite delivers an even distribution of crust, sauce, and toppings.

- Quick Cooking: Thinner dough requires less cooking time, making it perfect for weeknights or last-minute meals.

- Light and Versatile: Thin crusts can be paired with a wide range of toppings, from rich cheeses to fresh vegetables.

The Science of Ultra-Thin Crusts

Achieving an ultra-thin crust requires precision and attention to detail. Here are the key factors to consider:

1. Hydration Levels

- Thin-crust doughs generally have lower hydration (50-60%), resulting in a firmer, more pliable dough that can be rolled very thin.

2. Gluten Development

- Proper kneading or resting ensures enough gluten development for elasticity, allowing the dough to stretch without tearing.

3. Rolling vs. Stretching

- Thin crusts are often rolled out with a rolling pin for even thickness, unlike hand-stretched Neapolitan doughs.

4. Cooking Methods

- Thin crusts benefit from high heat to crisp the edges quickly without overcooking the toppings. A pizza stone or steel is ideal for even heat distribution.

Recipes for Flatbreads and Thin Crusts

1. Roman-Style Pizza

Roman-style pizza, known as "pizza al taglio," is baked in rectangular pans and features a thin, crispy crust that's sturdy enough to hold bold toppings.

Ingredients (Serves 4):

For the Dough:

- 3 1/2 cups all-purpose flour
- 1 teaspoon salt
- 1 teaspoon sugar
- 1 teaspoon active dry yeast
- 1 1/4 cups warm water
- 2 tablespoons olive oil

For the Toppings:

- 1/2 cup tomato sauce
- 8 ounces fresh mozzarella, sliced
- 1/2 cup artichoke hearts
- 1/4 cup black olives
- Fresh basil leaves

Instructions:

1. Prepare the Dough:

- Combine flour, salt, sugar, and yeast in a bowl. Add warm water and olive oil.
- Knead for 8-10 minutes until smooth. Let rise for 1 hour.

2. Preheat the Oven:

- Place a pizza stone in the oven and preheat to 500°F.

3. Roll Out the Dough:

- Roll the dough into a large rectangle and place it on a greased baking sheet.

4. Add Toppings:

- Spread a thin layer of tomato sauce. Top with mozzarella, artichokes, olives, and basil.

5. Bake:

- Transfer the baking sheet to the oven. Bake for 10-12 minutes until the crust is golden and crispy.

2. Crispy Cracker Crust Pizza

This ultra-thin crust is perfect for those who love a crunchy base that snaps with every bite.

Ingredients (Serves 4):

For the Dough:

- 2 cups all-purpose flour
- 1 teaspoon salt
- 1/2 teaspoon baking powder
- 1/2 cup water
- 2 tablespoons olive oil

For the Toppings:

- 1/2 cup tomato sauce
- 4 ounces shredded mozzarella
- 1/4 cup pepperoni slices
- Fresh oregano leaves

Instructions:

1. Make the Dough:

- Combine flour, salt, and baking powder. Add water and olive oil. Mix until a firm dough forms.
- Divide into two balls and rest for 15 minutes.

2. Preheat the Oven:

- Heat a pizza stone to 500°F.

3. Roll Out the Dough:

- Roll each ball into a thin circle, about 12 inches in diameter.

4. Add Toppings:

- Spread tomato sauce, sprinkle mozzarella, and add pepperoni.

5. Bake:

- Bake directly on the pizza stone for 8-10 minutes until crisp.

3. Lavash-Based Pizza

Lavash, a Middle Eastern flatbread, makes an excellent quick pizza base. It's light, crispy, and requires no preparation.

Ingredients (Serves 4):

For the Base:

- 2 large lavash flatbreads

For the Toppings:

- 1/4 cup pesto sauce
- 6 ounces grilled chicken, shredded
- 1/2 cup cherry tomatoes, halved
- 1/4 cup crumbled feta cheese
- Arugula for garnish

Instructions:

1. Preheat the Oven:

- Set the oven to 400°F.

2. Prepare the Flatbreads:

- Place lavash on a baking sheet. Spread a thin layer of pesto.

3. Add Toppings:

- Distribute chicken, tomatoes, and feta evenly.

4. Bake:

- Bake for 6-8 minutes until the edges are crispy.

5. Garnish:

- Top with fresh arugula before serving.

Mastering Ultra-Thin, Crispy Crusts

Achieving a perfect thin crust requires attention to detail. Here are some expert tips:

1. Use Low Hydration Dough

- Lower hydration creates a dough that's easier to roll thin and bakes into a crisp crust.

2. Roll Thinly

- Use a rolling pin to achieve an even thickness of 1/8 inch or less.

3. Preheat Your Oven

- Preheat a pizza stone or steel for at least 30 minutes at the highest temperature.

4. Avoid Overloading Toppings

- Too many toppings can weigh down the crust, making it soggy.

5. Finish with High Heat

- Thin crusts benefit from a quick, high-heat bake to develop crispness without drying out.

Pairing Light Toppings with Delicate Crusts

Thin crusts shine when paired with fresh, light ingredients. Here are some ideas:

1. Fresh Vegetables

- Thinly sliced zucchini, cherry tomatoes, and bell peppers work beautifully.

2. Light Cheeses

- Opt for fresh mozzarella, ricotta, or goat cheese.

3. Herb-Forward Sauces

- Pesto, garlic oil, or light tomato sauces enhance the flavors without overwhelming.

4. Minimal Proteins

- Use thinly sliced prosciutto, grilled chicken, or shrimp sparingly.

Conclusion: The Elegance of Thin Crusts

Flatbreads and thin crusts are a celebration of simplicity and balance, offering a crisp, light base for creative toppings. Whether you're making Roman-style pizza, cracker-thin crusts, or lavash-based creations, these styles invite you to experiment with flavors and textures. Their quick cooking time and adaptability make them a perfect choice for both casual meals and gourmet occasions.

In the next chapter, we'll explore the world of gourmet and artisanal pizzas, diving into techniques and recipes that elevate pizza-making into a true culinary art. Let's continue crafting pizzas that delight and inspire!

Chapter 8: Gourmet Pizzas

Gourmet pizzas represent the pinnacle of creativity and sophistication in pizza-making. With their luxurious toppings, bold flavor combinations, and elegant presentations, these pies are designed to elevate the humble pizza into an art form. Unlike traditional pizzas, which rely on simplicity and minimalism, gourmet pizzas embrace innovation, showcasing premium ingredients in ways that excite the palate.

This chapter explores the art of crafting gourmet pizzas, featuring standout recipes like truffle mushroom pizza, prosciutto and fig, and smoked salmon pizza. You'll also learn how to use high-quality ingredients, achieve balanced flavors, and create unforgettable gourmet experiences in your own kitchen.

The Appeal of Gourmet Pizzas

Gourmet pizzas stand out because they celebrate exceptional ingredients and innovative techniques. Here's what makes them unique:

- Premium Ingredients: From truffle oil to aged cheeses, gourmet pizzas use the finest components.
- Creative Flavors: They pair unexpected elements—savory and sweet, bold and delicate—for unforgettable taste experiences.
- Visual Elegance: Gourmet pizzas are as much about presentation as flavor, often served as centerpiece dishes.
- Versatility: Perfect for special occasions, dinner parties, or a refined twist on pizza night.

Essential Elements of Gourmet Pizza

1. High-Quality Ingredients

The success of gourmet pizzas hinges on ingredient quality. Invest in fresh, artisanal products to achieve restaurant-worthy results.

Key Ingredients to Elevate Your Pizza:

- Cheeses: Burrata, Gorgonzola, aged Parmesan, or triple-cream Brie.

- Truffle Products: Truffle oil, truffle salt, or fresh truffles for an earthy, luxurious touch.
- Cured Meats: Prosciutto, speck, or smoked salmon.
- Produce: Use seasonal fruits and vegetables for peak freshness.
- Herbs and Greens: Microgreens, arugula, and fresh herbs add flavor and sophistication.

2. Thin, Elegant Crusts

Gourmet pizzas often feature thin, crisp crusts that act as a delicate base for premium toppings.

- Use a pizza stone or steel to achieve an evenly baked crust.
- Focus on a light, airy dough with a subtle flavor that complements the toppings.

3. Balanced Flavor Profiles

Achieving a balance of flavors is critical for gourmet pizzas. Consider the following:

- Contrast: Pair salty cured meats with sweet fruits or honey.
- Richness: Balance creamy cheeses with acidic or bitter ingredients like lemon juice or arugula.
- Depth: Use umami-rich elements like mushrooms, aged cheeses, or anchovies to add complexity.

Gourmet Pizza Recipes

1. Truffle Mushroom Pizza

This earthy, decadent pizza combines the deep umami of mushrooms with the luxurious aroma of truffle oil.

Ingredients (Serves 4):

For the Dough:

- 2 Neapolitan pizza dough balls

For the Toppings:

- 1/2 cup white sauce (béchamel or garlic cream)
- 8 ounces mixed mushrooms (shiitake, cremini, oyster), sliced
- 2 tablespoons truffle oil
- 4 ounces fresh mozzarella, sliced
- 2 ounces grated Parmesan
- Fresh thyme leaves

Instructions:

1. Preheat the Oven: Heat a pizza stone to 500°F for 45 minutes.

2. Prepare the Mushrooms:

- Sauté mushrooms in olive oil over medium heat until tender. Season with salt and pepper.

3. Assemble the Pizza:

- Roll out the dough and spread a thin layer of white sauce.
- Scatter mozzarella slices and sautéed mushrooms evenly.
- Sprinkle Parmesan and fresh thyme.

4. Bake:

- Bake for 7-9 minutes until the crust is golden and the cheese is bubbling.

5. Finish:

- Drizzle with truffle oil and serve immediately.

Pro Tip: Add a poached egg in the center for an extra layer of richness.

2. Prosciutto and Fig Pizza

This pizza masterfully balances salty, sweet, and tangy flavors, making it a perfect choice for gourmet dining.

Ingredients (Serves 4):

For the Dough:

- 2 thin-crust dough balls

For the Toppings:

- 1/4 cup fig jam
- 4 ounces fresh mozzarella, sliced
- 4-6 thin slices of prosciutto
- 1/4 cup crumbled Gorgonzola

- Fresh arugula
- Honey for drizzling

Instructions:

1. Preheat the Oven: Heat a pizza stone to 500°F.
2. Assemble the Pizza:
- Roll out the dough and spread a thin layer of fig jam.
- Top with mozzarella slices and crumbled Gorgonzola.
3. Bake:
- Bake for 7-9 minutes until the crust is golden and the cheese is melted.
4. Add Finishing Touches:
- Arrange prosciutto slices and fresh arugula on top.
- Drizzle with honey for a hint of sweetness.

Pro Tip: Swap out fig jam for pear slices if figs are out of season.

3. Smoked Salmon Pizza

A luxurious, seafood-inspired pizza that's light, refreshing, and perfect for brunch or dinner parties.

Ingredients (Serves 4):

For the Dough:
- 2 thin-crust dough balls

For the Toppings:
- 1/4 cup crème fraîche
- 6 ounces smoked salmon, thinly sliced
- 1/4 cup capers
- 1/4 red onion, thinly sliced
- Fresh dill
- Lemon zest

Instructions:

1. Preheat the Oven: Heat a pizza stone to 500°F.
2. Prepare the Base:
- Roll out the dough and spread a thin layer of crème fraîche.
3. Bake the Crust:
- Bake for 5-7 minutes until lightly golden.
4. Add Toppings:

- Once the crust has cooled slightly, layer smoked salmon, capers, red onion, and dill.

- Sprinkle with lemon zest before serving.

Pro Tip: Serve with a side of chilled Prosecco for a touch of elegance.

Tips for Crafting Gourmet Pizzas

1. Highlight the Ingredients

- Let premium ingredients take center stage. Use minimal toppings to avoid overwhelming the palate.

2. Layer Thoughtfully

- Build your pizza with a balance of textures and flavors, starting with a complementary base (sauce or spread).

3. Finish with Fresh Elements

- Add greens, herbs, or drizzles (honey, balsamic reduction, or truffle oil) after baking for maximum impact.

4. Experiment with Presentation

- Arrange toppings artistically for a visually appealing pie that's ready for Instagram or a dinner party centerpiece.

5. Pair with Wine or Cocktails

- Enhance the experience by pairing your gourmet pizza with a complementary beverage.

- Truffle Mushroom Pizza: Pinot Noir or earthy red wines.

- Prosciutto and Fig Pizza: Sparkling wine or dry rosé.

- Smoked Salmon Pizza: Champagne or crisp white wines.

Elevating Pizza Night with Gourmet Creations

Gourmet pizzas are about more than just food—they're about crafting an experience. Whether you're hosting friends, celebrating a special occasion, or simply treating yourself, these elevated pies turn pizza night into something extraordinary.

In the next chapter, we'll dive into vegetarian and vegan options, exploring how plant-based ingredients can create satisfying, innovative pizzas. Let's continue pushing the boundaries of pizza-making!

Chapter 9: Vegetarian and Vegan Pizzas

Pizza is one of the most versatile dishes in the culinary world, and vegetarian and vegan options offer endless opportunities for creativity. From vibrant roasted vegetables to creamy plant-based cheeses, vegetarian and vegan pizzas can be just as hearty and satisfying as their traditional counterparts. Whether you're embracing a plant-based lifestyle, catering to dietary preferences, or simply looking for healthier options, vegetarian and vegan pizzas can deliver bold flavors and nutritional benefits.

In this chapter, we'll dive into the art of creating vegetarian and vegan pizzas, featuring recipes like roasted vegetable medley, vegan Margherita, and cauliflower crust pizza. You'll also learn tips for incorporating vegan cheeses, meat substitutes, and fresh produce to craft delicious, plant-forward pizzas.

The Appeal of Vegetarian and Vegan Pizzas

Why Choose Plant-Based Pizzas?

Vegetarian and vegan pizzas are not just about eliminating meat or dairy—they're about celebrating the vibrant flavors and textures of plant-based ingredients.

1. Health Benefits: Packed with vegetables, whole grains, and plant-based proteins, these pizzas offer a nutritious alternative.

2. Sustainability: Choosing plant-based options reduces your carbon footprint and supports eco-friendly practices.

3. Versatility: Vegetables, legumes, and vegan alternatives provide endless combinations for creative toppings.

4. Inclusivity: Vegetarian and vegan pizzas cater to a wide range of dietary needs, making them perfect for gatherings and shared meals.

The Essentials of Vegetarian and Vegan Pizza

1. The Crust

A great pizza starts with the crust. While traditional dough is naturally vegan, there are innovative crust options to explore:

- Classic Dough: Made with flour, water, yeast, and salt, this is a simple and reliable base.

- Whole Wheat Dough: Adds fiber and a nutty flavor.

- Cauliflower Crust: A low-carb, gluten-free alternative with a crispy texture.

- Sweet Potato Crust: Slightly sweet and nutrient-dense, this crust pairs well with savory toppings.

2. The Sauce

Vegetarian and vegan pizzas allow for endless creativity with sauces:

- Classic Tomato Sauce: Naturally vegan and perfect for traditional pies.

- Pesto: Swap Parmesan for nutritional yeast to make it vegan.

- Garlic Cream Sauce: Use cashews or plant-based milk for a dairy-free version.

- Hummus or Bean Purees: Offer a protein-packed alternative.

3. The Cheese

Vegan cheeses have come a long way, with options that melt, stretch, and taste like dairy-based cheeses.

- Cashew Cheese: Creamy and tangy, ideal for dolloping or spreading.

- Coconut Oil-Based Cheese: Brands like Violife and Daiya offer excellent melting properties.

- Nut-Free Options: Made from tapioca starch, potatoes, or soy for allergen-friendly choices.

- Nutritional Yeast: Adds a cheesy flavor when sprinkled on top.

4. Plant-Based Proteins

Incorporating plant-based proteins ensures your pizza is hearty and satisfying:

- Legumes: Chickpeas, lentils, and black beans add protein and texture.

- Tofu: Crumbled, marinated, or baked tofu works well as a topping.

- Seitan and Tempeh: Meat substitutes that mimic the texture of traditional proteins.

- Vegan Sausages or Pepperoni: Pre-made options from brands like Beyond Meat or Field Roast.

Recipes for Vegetarian and Vegan Pizzas

1. Roasted Vegetable Medley Pizza

This vibrant pizza showcases the natural sweetness and depth of roasted vegetables.

Ingredients (Serves 4):

For the Dough:

- 1 classic pizza dough ball

For the Toppings:

- 1/2 cup tomato sauce
- 1 cup roasted vegetables (bell peppers, zucchini, eggplant, red onion)
- 4 ounces mozzarella (or vegan cheese of choice)
- Fresh basil leaves
- Olive oil

Instructions:

1. Preheat the Oven: Heat a pizza stone or steel to 500°F.

2. Prepare the Vegetables:

- Toss sliced vegetables with olive oil, salt, and pepper. Roast at 400°F for 20 minutes until tender and slightly caramelized.

3. Assemble the Pizza:

- Roll out the dough and spread a thin layer of tomato sauce.
- Scatter roasted vegetables and mozzarella evenly.

4. Bake:

- Bake for 7-9 minutes until the crust is golden and the cheese is bubbling.

5. Finish:

- Garnish with fresh basil and a drizzle of olive oil before serving.

2. Vegan Margherita Pizza

A plant-based twist on the classic, this pizza is simple, elegant, and packed with flavor.

Ingredients (Serves 4):

For the Dough:

- 1 classic pizza dough ball

For the Toppings:

- 1/2 cup tomato sauce
- 4 ounces vegan mozzarella (or cashew cheese)
- Fresh basil leaves
- Olive oil

Instructions:

1. Preheat the Oven: Heat a pizza stone or steel to 500°F.
2. Assemble the Pizza:
- Roll out the dough and spread a thin layer of tomato sauce.
- Add slices of vegan mozzarella evenly.
3. Bake:
- Bake for 7-9 minutes until the crust is golden and the cheese is melted.
4. Finish:
- Add fresh basil leaves and drizzle with olive oil before serving.

Pro Tip: Use nutritional yeast for an additional cheesy flavor.

3. Cauliflower Crust Pizza

This low-carb, gluten-free option is light, crispy, and packed with nutrients.

Ingredients (Serves 4):

For the Crust:

- 1 medium cauliflower head, grated
- 1/4 cup almond flour
- 1/4 cup nutritional yeast
- 1 flax egg (1 tablespoon ground flaxseed + 3 tablespoons water)
- 1 teaspoon salt

For the Toppings:

- 1/2 cup pesto (vegan)
- 1/2 cup cherry tomatoes, halved

- 1/4 cup pine nuts
- Fresh arugula

Instructions:

1. Prepare the Crust:
- Preheat the oven to 425°F.
- Steam grated cauliflower for 5 minutes, then squeeze out excess moisture using a clean towel.
- Mix cauliflower with almond flour, nutritional yeast, flax egg, and salt.
- Form a dough and press into a 10-inch circle on parchment paper.

2. Bake the Crust:
- Bake for 15-20 minutes until firm and golden.

3. Add Toppings:
- Spread pesto, add cherry tomatoes, and sprinkle pine nuts.

4. Bake Again:
- Bake for 5-7 minutes until toppings are warm.

5. Finish:
- Top with fresh arugula before serving.

Tips for Creating Hearty, Satisfying Plant-Based Pizzas

1. Focus on Texture
- Use a combination of crunchy, creamy, and chewy elements for a balanced bite.

2. Layer Flavors
- Pair earthy vegetables with tangy sauces or spicy toppings for depth.

3. Use Seasonal Ingredients
- Fresh, in-season produce ensures maximum flavor and nutritional value.

4. Experiment with Bases
- Try alternative crusts like sweet potato, polenta, or whole grain for variety.

5. Customize Proteins
- Marinate tofu or tempeh in bold flavors like barbecue or teriyaki for added interest.

Incorporating Vegan Cheeses and Meat Substitutes

Cheese Tips

1. Blend Cheeses: Mix different vegan cheeses for improved flavor and melting properties.

2. Add Post-Bake: For maximum creaminess, dollop soft vegan cheeses after baking.

Meat Substitute Tips

1. Choose Wisely: Opt for high-quality brands like Beyond Meat or homemade alternatives.

2. Pre-Cook: Cook plant-based meats before adding to ensure texture and flavor.

Conclusion: A Celebration of Plant-Based Creativity

Vegetarian and vegan pizzas are an invitation to experiment with bold flavors, fresh ingredients, and innovative techniques. From the earthy richness of roasted vegetables to the creamy decadence of plant-based cheeses, these pizzas prove that plant-forward eating can be both satisfying and delicious.

In the next chapter, we'll dive into the world of dessert pizzas, exploring sweet creations that transform pizza into the ultimate indulgence. Let's continue crafting pizzas that surprise and delight!

Chapter 10: Global Pizza Inspirations

Pizza is one of the most beloved foods worldwide, and its versatility has allowed it to be reinvented in countless ways across different cultures. From spicy Thai chicken to aromatic Middle Eastern za'atar, global pizza variations demonstrate how traditional pizza techniques can beautifully harmonize with diverse cuisines. By blending classic dough and baking methods with regional ingredients, these pizzas bring together the best of both worlds.

In this chapter, we'll explore how to infuse your pizzas with international flavors through recipes like Thai chicken pizza, Indian tikka pizza, and Middle Eastern za'atar pizza. Along the way, you'll learn how to adapt traditional techniques and ingredients to create exciting, globally inspired pizzas.

The Allure of Global Pizza Flavors

Why Explore International Pizza?

1. Cultural Exploration: Global pizzas are a delicious way to experience the flavors of other cuisines.

2. Creative Fusion: Merging traditional pizza methods with international ingredients sparks culinary innovation.

3. Versatility: Pizza serves as a blank canvas, allowing for endless experimentation with new flavors and textures.

Blending Traditional Techniques with Global Cuisines

The key to crafting globally inspired pizzas is balancing authentic regional flavors with the structure and method of classic pizza-making. Here's how to approach this culinary fusion:

1. Start with the Dough

- Use traditional pizza dough as a base. Its neutral flavor and elasticity pair well with bold, flavorful toppings.

2. Adapt the Sauce

- Replace standard tomato sauce with region-specific bases like curry, peanut sauce, or tahini.

3. Customize Toppings

- Incorporate ingredients native to the cuisine you're highlighting, such as paneer, kimchi, or za'atar.

4. Finish with Authentic Garnishes

- Add herbs, oils, or spices after baking to enhance the flavor profile. Examples include cilantro, sesame oil, or mint leaves.

Recipes for Global Pizza Inspirations

1. Thai Chicken Pizza

This pizza brings the vibrant, spicy, and tangy flavors of Thai cuisine to your table. A peanut sauce base pairs beautifully with marinated chicken, fresh vegetables, and zesty garnishes.

Ingredients (Serves 4):

For the Dough:

- 1 classic pizza dough ball

For the Peanut Sauce Base:

- 1/4 cup creamy peanut butter
- 2 tablespoons soy sauce
- 1 tablespoon rice vinegar
- 1 teaspoon sesame oil
- 1 teaspoon sriracha (adjust for spice level)
- 1 tablespoon water (to thin, if necessary)

For the Toppings:

- 1 cup cooked, shredded chicken (marinated in lime juice, soy sauce, and garlic)
- 1/2 cup shredded mozzarella
- 1/2 cup julienned carrots
- 1/2 cup thinly sliced red bell peppers
- 1/4 cup chopped green onions
- 2 tablespoons chopped peanuts

- Fresh cilantro for garnish

Instructions:

1. Preheat the Oven: Heat a pizza stone to 500°F.

2. Prepare the Sauce:

- Whisk together all peanut sauce ingredients until smooth.

3. Assemble the Pizza:

- Roll out the dough and spread a thin layer of peanut sauce.
- Add shredded chicken, mozzarella, carrots, and red bell peppers.

4. Bake:

- Bake for 7-9 minutes until the crust is golden and the cheese is melted.

5. Finish:

- Garnish with green onions, peanuts, and cilantro before serving.

Pro Tip: Add a drizzle of sriracha or a squeeze of lime for an extra burst of flavor.

2. Indian Tikka Pizza

Infused with the bold spices of Indian cuisine, this pizza features a tikka masala base, tender pieces of paneer or chicken, and a cooling yogurt drizzle.

Ingredients (Serves 4):

For the Dough:

- 1 whole wheat pizza dough ball

For the Tikka Masala Sauce:

- 1/2 cup tikka masala sauce (store-bought or homemade)
- 1/4 cup coconut milk

For the Toppings:

- 1 cup marinated paneer or chicken tikka (grilled or baked)
- 1/2 cup red onions, thinly sliced
- 1/2 cup diced tomatoes
- 4 ounces shredded mozzarella or crumbled feta
- Fresh cilantro for garnish

For the Yogurt Drizzle:

- 1/4 cup plain yogurt
- 1 teaspoon lemon juice
- Pinch of cumin

Instructions:

1. Preheat the Oven: Heat a pizza stone to 500°F.

2. Prepare the Sauce:

- Mix tikka masala sauce with coconut milk for a creamy, flavorful base.

3. Assemble the Pizza:

- Roll out the dough and spread a thin layer of tikka masala sauce.
- Top with paneer or chicken, red onions, tomatoes, and mozzarella.

4. Bake:

- Bake for 8-10 minutes until the crust is golden and the cheese is bubbling.

5. Finish:

- Drizzle with yogurt sauce and garnish with fresh cilantro.

Pro Tip: For extra spice, sprinkle chili flakes or garam masala before serving.

3. Middle Eastern Za'atar Pizza

Aromatic and earthy, this pizza highlights za'atar—a Middle Eastern spice blend—paired with fresh vegetables, tangy labneh, and olive oil.

Ingredients (Serves 4):

For the Dough:

- 1 flatbread-style dough ball

For the Za'atar Spread:

- 3 tablespoons za'atar spice mix
- 2 tablespoons olive oil

For the Toppings:

- 1/2 cup cherry tomatoes, halved
- 1/4 cup sliced black olives
- 1/4 cup thinly sliced red onions
- 1/4 cup crumbled feta
- Fresh mint leaves

For the Labneh Drizzle:

- 1/4 cup labneh or Greek yogurt
- 1 teaspoon lemon juice

Instructions:

1. Preheat the Oven: Heat a pizza stone to 500°F.

2. Prepare the Za'atar Spread:
- Mix za'atar with olive oil to create a paste.
3. Assemble the Pizza:
- Roll out the dough and spread the za'atar mixture evenly.
- Top with cherry tomatoes, olives, red onions, and feta.
4. Bake:
- Bake for 7-9 minutes until the crust is crispy.
5. Finish:
- Drizzle with labneh sauce and garnish with fresh mint.

Pro Tip: Serve with a side of hummus or baba ghanoush for a complete Middle Eastern feast.

Exploring International Ingredients and Toppings

1. Key Ingredients by Cuisine
- Thai: Coconut milk, lemongrass, fish sauce, and fresh herbs like cilantro and basil.
- Indian: Garam masala, cumin, yogurt, paneer, and mint.
- Middle Eastern: Za'atar, tahini, labneh, pomegranate seeds, and sumac.
2. Pairing Sauces with Cuisines
- Spicy Peanut Sauce: Perfect for Thai or Southeast Asian flavors.
- Curry Bases: Ideal for Indian-inspired pizzas.
- Olive Oil and Herb Blends: Best for Mediterranean or Middle Eastern pizzas.
3. Using Garnishes for Authenticity
- Fresh herbs, lemon zest, and toasted seeds add brightness and texture to global pizzas.

Tips for Perfect Global Pizzas

1. Balance Flavors: Ensure a mix of sweet, savory, spicy, and tangy elements for a complex flavor profile.

2. Focus on Freshness: Use seasonal, high-quality ingredients for authentic results.

3. Don't Overload Toppings: Highlight key flavors without overwhelming the crust.

4. Experiment with Sauces: Adapt traditional pizza sauces to complement global ingredients.

Conclusion: A World of Pizza Awaits

Global pizzas celebrate the diverse culinary traditions of the world, bringing bold flavors and new experiences to your table. By blending classic pizza-making techniques with regional ingredients and recipes, you can create delicious, one-of-a-kind pies that transport you to new destinations with every bite.

In the next chapter, we'll explore dessert pizzas, transforming pizza into a decadent, sweet treat for any occasion. Let's continue this flavorful journey!

Chapter 11: Breakfast and Brunch Pizzas

Pizza isn't just for lunch or dinner anymore—its versatility makes it a perfect canvas for morning flavors as well. Breakfast and brunch pizzas bring together the best of two culinary worlds, transforming traditional breakfast ingredients like eggs, bacon, and avocado into exciting pizza creations. Whether you're hosting a weekend brunch, looking for a unique breakfast option, or satisfying a late-morning craving, breakfast and brunch pizzas are a crowd-pleasing choice.

This chapter explores how to adapt pizza for morning meals, offering standout recipes like egg and bacon pizza, avocado toast pizza, and smoked salmon bagel pizza. You'll also learn how to pair breakfast toppings with savory crusts for a perfectly balanced start to your day.

Why Breakfast and Brunch Pizzas Work

1. The Versatility of Pizza

Pizza is a blank canvas, and its ability to accommodate a variety of toppings makes it an excellent vehicle for breakfast flavors.

2. A Hearty Start

Breakfast pizzas combine protein, carbs, and fresh ingredients, making them a satisfying way to kick off the day.

3. Customizable for Any Taste

From rich and indulgent options like bacon and cheese to lighter, veggie-forward versions, there's a breakfast pizza for everyone.

Crafting the Perfect Morning Pizza

1. Choosing the Right Dough

- Traditional Dough: Classic pizza dough works well for a hearty, satisfying breakfast base.
- Whole Wheat or Sourdough: These add a rustic, nutty flavor that pairs beautifully with savory breakfast toppings.
- Thin Crust or Flatbread: Ideal for lighter brunch pizzas.

2. Sauce Options for Breakfast

- Tomato Sauce: Works well for traditional flavors like bacon and egg.

- White Sauce: A creamy béchamel or ricotta spread complements ingredients like smoked salmon or mushrooms.

- Avocado or Pesto: These vibrant sauces bring freshness to lighter options.

3. Toppings That Shine in the Morning

- Proteins: Eggs, bacon, sausage, smoked salmon, tofu, or tempeh for plant-based options.

- Vegetables: Spinach, tomatoes, mushrooms, or bell peppers for added nutrients and color.

- Cheeses: Mozzarella, cheddar, goat cheese, or cream cheese depending on the flavor profile.

Breakfast and Brunch Pizza Recipes

1. Egg and Bacon Pizza

This classic breakfast pizza combines crispy bacon, sunny-side-up eggs, and melted cheese for a hearty morning meal.

Ingredients (Serves 4):

For the Dough:

- 1 classic pizza dough ball

For the Toppings:

- 1/2 cup tomato sauce
- 1 cup shredded mozzarella
- 4 slices of cooked bacon, chopped
- 4 eggs
- 1/4 cup grated Parmesan
- Fresh chives for garnish

Instructions:

1. Preheat the Oven: Heat a pizza stone or steel to 500°F.

2. Assemble the Pizza:

- Roll out the dough and spread a thin layer of tomato sauce.
- Sprinkle mozzarella evenly. Add chopped bacon.

3. Bake:

- Bake for 6-8 minutes until the crust begins to set.

4. Add Eggs:

- Carefully crack the eggs onto the pizza, spacing them evenly.

- Bake for another 3-4 minutes until the egg whites are set but the yolks are runny.

5. Finish:

- Sprinkle Parmesan and fresh chives before serving.

Pro Tip: Use pre-cooked bacon to avoid excess grease.

2. Avocado Toast Pizza

A fresh, modern twist on the beloved avocado toast, this pizza is perfect for lighter brunch gatherings.

Ingredients (Serves 4):

For the Dough:

- 1 whole wheat pizza dough ball

For the Toppings:

- 1/2 cup smashed avocado (seasoned with salt, pepper, and lemon juice)
- 1/2 cup cherry tomatoes, halved
- 1/4 cup crumbled feta cheese
- 2 soft-boiled eggs, sliced
- Arugula for garnish

Instructions:

1. Preheat the Oven: Heat a pizza stone to 500°F.

2. Bake the Crust:

- Roll out the dough and bake it plain for 7-8 minutes until lightly golden.

3. Add Toppings:

- Spread smashed avocado over the crust.
- Top with cherry tomatoes, feta, and sliced eggs.

4. Finish:

- Garnish with arugula and drizzle with olive oil before serving.

Pro Tip: Add red chili flakes for a spicy kick.

3. Smoked Salmon Bagel Pizza

Combining the flavors of a bagel with lox, this pizza features smoked salmon, cream cheese, and capers for an elegant brunch option.

Ingredients (Serves 4):

For the Dough:

- 1 flatbread-style dough ball

For the Toppings:

- 1/4 cup cream cheese (softened)
- 6 ounces smoked salmon
- 1/4 cup capers
- 1/4 red onion, thinly sliced
- Fresh dill for garnish
- Lemon wedges for serving

Instructions:

1. Preheat the Oven: Heat the oven to 450°F.
2. Bake the Crust:

- Roll out the dough and bake it plain for 6-7 minutes until crisp.

3. Add Toppings:

- Spread cream cheese evenly over the cooled crust.
- Arrange smoked salmon, capers, and red onion slices.

4. Finish:

- Garnish with dill and serve with lemon wedges.

Pro Tip: Serve with a side of sparkling water or mimosa for a complete brunch experience.

Tips for Adapting Pizza for Morning Meals

1. Prep Ingredients Ahead

- Cook proteins like bacon or sausage in advance to save time.

2. Focus on Balance

- Pair rich ingredients like cheese or eggs with fresh elements like greens or tomatoes for a lighter feel.

3. Keep the Crust Versatile

- Adjust the crust's thickness depending on the desired texture: thinner for light brunches, thicker for hearty breakfasts.

4. Experiment with Sweet and Savory

- Add a touch of sweetness with honey, maple syrup, or caramelized onions to balance savory toppings.

5. Pair with Morning Beverages

- Complement your pizza with coffee, tea, or fresh juice to enhance the breakfast experience.

Creative Topping Ideas for Breakfast Pizzas

1. Sweet Potato and Kale: A healthy option with roasted sweet potato cubes, sautéed kale, and goat cheese.

2. Mushroom and Spinach: Earthy mushrooms and wilted spinach with a drizzle of truffle oil.

3. Plant-Based Breakfast Pizza: Vegan sausage, tofu scramble, and nutritional yeast for a protein-packed start.

4. Fruit and Cheese: Combine ricotta, honey, and figs for a sweet brunch option.

Conclusion: The Morning Evolution of Pizza

Breakfast and brunch pizzas are a testament to the versatility of pizza, offering unique ways to bring morning flavors to life. Whether you're indulging in a savory egg and bacon pie, savoring the freshness of avocado toast, or treating yourself to the elegance of smoked salmon, these pizzas are guaranteed to start your day deliciously.

In the next chapter, we'll explore dessert pizzas, turning this savory classic into a sweet, decadent treat perfect for any occasion. Let's continue this journey through the endless possibilities of pizza!

Chapter 12: Dessert Pizzas

Pizza is often associated with savory flavors, but dessert pizzas open up a world of possibilities for indulgent, sweet creations. By reimagining the classic pizza concept with sweet doughs, luscious glazes, and decadent toppings, dessert pizzas offer a unique way to satisfy your sweet tooth. Perfect for parties, family gatherings, or simply treating yourself, these delightful creations combine the comfort of pizza with the joy of dessert.

In this chapter, we'll explore the art of crafting dessert pizzas with recipes like Nutella and banana pizza, s'mores pizza, and fruit tart pizza. You'll learn how to create sweet doughs and glazes, balance flavors and textures, and experiment with toppings to create show-stopping desserts.

The Concept of Dessert Pizzas

Why Dessert Pizzas Work

1. Versatility: Dessert pizzas can be customized with various toppings, from fresh fruit to rich chocolates and nuts.

2. Balance: The combination of a slightly crisp base with sweet, creamy, and crunchy toppings offers a perfect textural contrast.

3. Presentation: Dessert pizzas are visually stunning, making them ideal for entertaining.

Key Elements of a Dessert Pizza

1. The Base: A slightly sweetened dough or alternative crust sets the stage for the toppings.

2. The Sauce: Instead of tomato sauce, dessert pizzas use spreads like Nutella, cream cheese, or fruit preserves.

3. The Toppings: Fresh fruit, chocolates, marshmallows, and nuts are popular choices.

4. The Finish: A drizzle of glaze, powdered sugar, or a sprinkle of spices adds the final touch.

Crafting Sweet Doughs and Glazes

1. Sweet Pizza Dough

A good dessert pizza starts with a well-crafted sweet dough. While it should resemble traditional pizza dough in texture, it includes a touch of sugar or honey for sweetness.

Sweet Dough Recipe (Makes 2 Medium Pizzas):

Ingredients:

- 2 1/4 teaspoons active dry yeast
- 1/4 cup warm water
- 3 cups all-purpose flour
- 1/4 cup sugar
- 1/4 teaspoon salt
- 1/2 cup milk, warmed
- 1/4 cup unsalted butter, melted
- 1 large egg

Instructions:

1. Activate Yeast: Dissolve yeast in warm water with a pinch of sugar. Let sit for 5 minutes until frothy.

2. Mix Ingredients: Combine flour, sugar, and salt in a large bowl. Add milk, butter, egg, and yeast mixture. Mix until a dough forms.

3. Knead Dough: Knead on a floured surface for 8-10 minutes until smooth and elastic.

4. Let Rise: Place the dough in a greased bowl, cover, and let rise in a warm place for 1-2 hours until doubled in size.

2. Glazes for Dessert Pizzas

A glaze adds moisture, sweetness, and visual appeal to dessert pizzas. Here are some popular options:

Cream Cheese Glaze

- 4 ounces cream cheese, softened
- 1/4 cup powdered sugar

- 2 tablespoons milk
- 1/2 teaspoon vanilla extract

Mix until smooth and drizzle over baked pizzas.

Chocolate Ganache

- 1/2 cup heavy cream
- 1 cup chopped dark chocolate

Heat the cream and pour it over the chocolate. Stir until smooth and glossy.

Fruit Glaze

- 1/4 cup fruit preserves (apricot, strawberry, or peach)
- 2 tablespoons water

Heat together and brush over fresh fruit toppings for shine.

Dessert Pizza Recipes

1. Nutella and Banana Pizza

A classic combination of creamy chocolate and sweet bananas, this pizza is a crowd-pleaser for chocolate lovers.

Ingredients (Serves 4):

For the Dough:

- 1 sweet pizza dough ball

For the Toppings:

- 1/2 cup Nutella
- 2 bananas, thinly sliced
- 1/4 cup chopped hazelnuts
- Powdered sugar for dusting

Instructions:

1. Preheat the Oven: Heat a pizza stone to 450°F.

2. Prepare the Dough:

- Roll out the dough into a 12-inch circle. Bake plain for 7-8 minutes until lightly golden.

3. Add Nutella:

- Spread Nutella over the warm crust.

4. Top with Bananas and Hazelnuts:

- Arrange banana slices and sprinkle chopped hazelnuts.

5. Finish:

- Dust with powdered sugar before serving.

Pro Tip: Add a scoop of vanilla ice cream for an extra indulgent treat.

2. S'mores Pizza

This pizza transforms the campfire favorite into a gooey, decadent dessert.

Ingredients (Serves 4):

For the Dough:

- 1 sweet pizza dough ball

For the Toppings:

- 1/2 cup chocolate chips
- 1/2 cup mini marshmallows
- 1/4 cup crushed graham crackers

Instructions:

1. Preheat the Oven: Heat a pizza stone to 450°F.

2. Prepare the Dough:

- Roll out the dough into a 12-inch circle. Bake plain for 6-7 minutes until slightly firm.

3. Add Toppings:

- Sprinkle chocolate chips and marshmallows evenly over the crust.

4. Bake Again:

- Return to the oven for 2-3 minutes until the marshmallows are golden and gooey.

5. Finish:

- Sprinkle crushed graham crackers over the top before serving.

Pro Tip: Use a kitchen torch for perfectly toasted marshmallows.

3. Fruit Tart Pizza

This elegant dessert pizza showcases a colorful array of fresh fruits on a creamy base.

Ingredients (Serves 4):

For the Dough:

- 1 sweet pizza dough ball

For the Base:

- 1/2 cup cream cheese glaze

For the Toppings:

- 1/2 cup sliced strawberries
- 1/4 cup blueberries
- 1 kiwi, peeled and sliced
- 1/4 cup mango slices
- 2 tablespoons apricot glaze

Instructions:

1. Preheat the Oven: Heat a pizza stone to 450°F.

2. Prepare the Dough:

- Roll out the dough into a 12-inch circle. Bake plain for 7-8 minutes until lightly golden.

3. Add the Cream Cheese Base:

- Spread cream cheese glaze over the cooled crust.

4. Arrange the Fruit:

- Artistically arrange the sliced fruits over the glaze.

5. Finish:

- Brush the fruit with apricot glaze for shine.

Pro Tip: Serve chilled for a refreshing dessert.

Balancing Sweetness and Texture

1. The Crust

- Ensure the crust is not overly sweet to avoid overwhelming the toppings. A subtle sweetness works best.

2. The Sauce

- Match the sweetness of the sauce to the toppings. Rich spreads like Nutella pair well with neutral bases, while tart fruit glazes complement sweet crusts.

3. The Toppings

- Combine creamy, crunchy, and juicy elements for a dynamic bite.

4. The Finish

- A sprinkle of powdered sugar, drizzle of caramel, or fresh mint garnish adds visual appeal and extra flavor.

Tips for Crafting Dessert Pizzas

1. Experiment with Alternative Crusts: Use cookie dough, brownie batter, or puff pastry for creative bases.

2. Use Seasonal Fruits: Fresh, ripe fruits elevate the flavor and presentation of dessert pizzas.

3. Control Sweetness: Avoid overly sweet combinations by balancing rich and tart elements.

4. Serve Fresh: Most dessert pizzas are best enjoyed immediately after preparation.

Conclusion: Transforming Pizza into Dessert Perfection

Dessert pizzas are a testament to the versatility of pizza, turning a savory favorite into a sweet masterpiece. Whether you're indulging in a rich Nutella and banana creation, savoring the nostalgia of a s'mores pizza, or delighting in the elegance of a fruit tart pizza, these recipes offer something for every occasion. With the tips and techniques in this chapter, you can create dessert pizzas that dazzle your guests and satisfy any sweet craving.

In the next chapter, we'll dive into tips for hosting a pizza party, from planning toppings to creating interactive experiences for guests. Let's continue this journey into the endless possibilities of pizza!

Chapter 13: Gluten-Free and Low-Carb Pizzas

As dietary preferences evolve, gluten-free and low-carb pizzas have become increasingly popular. These pizzas provide options for those with gluten intolerance, celiac disease, or individuals following low-carb or keto lifestyles. By using alternative flours, creative ingredients, and innovative techniques, you can craft delicious pizzas that cater to a variety of dietary needs without sacrificing flavor or texture.

In this chapter, we'll explore the art of making gluten-free and low-carb pizzas, featuring recipes like cauliflower crust pizza, almond flour crust pizza, and other keto-friendly options. We'll also dive into the techniques for working with non-traditional doughs and share tips for mastering alternative ingredients.

Why Choose Gluten-Free or Low-Carb Pizzas?

Health and Dietary Benefits

1. Gluten Sensitivity: Ideal for those with celiac disease or gluten intolerance.
2. Low-Carb Diets: Supports ketogenic and other low-carb lifestyles by reducing carbohydrate intake.
3. Nutritional Boost: Incorporating vegetables, nuts, and seeds into pizza crusts can increase the overall nutritional value.

Flavorful Alternatives

Non-traditional crusts often bring unique flavors and textures to the table, enhancing the overall pizza experience.

Challenges of Gluten-Free and Low-Carb Doughs

Working with gluten-free and low-carb doughs requires understanding the properties of alternative ingredients.

1. No Gluten Structure: Without gluten, dough lacks elasticity, which can make it harder to handle.

2. Texture Variability: Gluten-free flours can produce a crumbly or dense texture if not balanced properly.

3. Moisture Management: Alternative flours often absorb water differently, affecting consistency.

Mastering Non-Traditional Pizza Doughs

1. Choosing the Right Ingredients

- Cauliflower: A versatile base for low-carb crusts.
- Almond Flour: Adds a nutty flavor and soft texture.
- Coconut Flour: Absorbs moisture and adds a slight sweetness.
- Tapioca Starch: Helps bind gluten-free doughs.
- Cheese and Eggs: Often used as binders in keto-friendly crusts.

2. Techniques for Perfect Gluten-Free and Low-Carb Doughs

1. Balance Ingredients: Combine flours and starches to achieve a cohesive texture.

2. Pre-Bake Crusts: Many gluten-free and low-carb crusts need to be pre-baked to ensure firmness before adding toppings.

3. Use Parchment Paper: Prevents sticking and makes handling dough easier.

4. Keep It Thin: Thinner crusts are easier to bake evenly and maintain structure.

Recipes for Gluten-Free and Low-Carb Pizzas

1. Cauliflower Crust Pizza

This popular low-carb option uses cauliflower as the base, creating a light, crispy crust that pairs well with a variety of toppings.

Ingredients (Serves 4):

For the Crust:

- 1 medium cauliflower head, grated
- 1/4 cup grated Parmesan cheese
- 1/4 cup shredded mozzarella cheese
- 1 large egg
- 1/2 teaspoon salt
- 1/2 teaspoon garlic powder

For the Toppings:

- 1/2 cup tomato sauce
- 1 cup shredded mozzarella cheese
- 1/2 cup sliced vegetables (bell peppers, mushrooms, olives)
- Fresh basil for garnish

Instructions:

1. Prepare the Cauliflower:

- Steam grated cauliflower for 5 minutes, then squeeze out excess moisture using a clean kitchen towel.

2. Make the Dough:

- Mix cauliflower with Parmesan, mozzarella, egg, salt, and garlic powder until well combined.

3. Pre-Bake the Crust:

- Spread the mixture onto a parchment-lined baking sheet, shaping it into a 10-inch circle.
- Bake at 400°F for 15-20 minutes until golden and firm.

4. Add Toppings:

- Spread tomato sauce, sprinkle mozzarella, and add vegetables.

5. Bake Again:

- Bake for another 10 minutes until the cheese is melted and bubbly.

Pro Tip: Let the crust cool slightly before slicing to maintain its structure.

2. Almond Flour Crust Pizza

Almond flour creates a soft, nutty crust that's naturally gluten-free and low in carbohydrates.

Ingredients (Serves 4):

For the Crust:
- 2 cups almond flour
- 1/4 teaspoon salt
- 1 teaspoon baking powder
- 2 large eggs
- 2 tablespoons olive oil

For the Toppings:
- 1/4 cup pesto sauce
- 1/2 cup cherry tomatoes, halved
- 1/4 cup crumbled feta cheese
- Fresh arugula for garnish

Instructions:

1. Make the Dough:
- Mix almond flour, salt, and baking powder in a bowl.
- Add eggs and olive oil, stirring until a dough forms.

2. Shape the Crust:
- Press the dough onto a parchment-lined baking sheet, shaping it into a 10-inch circle.

3. Pre-Bake the Crust:
- Bake at 375°F for 10-12 minutes until slightly golden.

4. Add Toppings:
- Spread pesto sauce, add cherry tomatoes, and sprinkle feta cheese.

5. Bake Again:
- Bake for another 8-10 minutes until toppings are warmed through.

Pro Tip: Garnish with fresh arugula for a peppery finish.

3. Keto-Friendly Cheese Crust Pizza

This crust is made entirely of cheese and eggs, offering a rich, indulgent option for keto followers.

Ingredients (Serves 4):

For the Crust:
- 2 cups shredded mozzarella cheese
- 2 large eggs
- 1/2 teaspoon Italian seasoning

For the Toppings:

- 1/2 cup tomato sauce (low-carb)
- 1 cup shredded mozzarella cheese
- 1/4 cup sliced pepperoni

Instructions:

1. Make the Dough:

- Mix shredded mozzarella, eggs, and Italian seasoning in a bowl until combined.

2. Shape the Crust:

- Spread the mixture onto a parchment-lined baking sheet, forming a thin circle.

3. Bake the Crust:

- Bake at 375°F for 12-15 minutes until firm and golden.

4. Add Toppings:

- Spread tomato sauce, sprinkle mozzarella, and add pepperoni.

5. Bake Again:

- Bake for another 8-10 minutes until the cheese is melted and bubbly.

Pro Tip: Let the crust cool slightly before cutting to ensure clean slices.

Tips for Working with Alternative Ingredients

1. Use a Food Processor: Helps create a fine texture for ingredients like cauliflower or nuts.

2. Balance Wet and Dry Ingredients: Too much moisture can make the crust soggy, while too little can cause cracking.

3. Experiment with Binders: Eggs, flaxseeds, and psyllium husk are effective for holding dough together.

4. Adjust Cooking Times: Alternative flours and crusts often require pre-baking or longer cook times.

Alternative Flour Blends for Gluten-Free Pizzas

For those looking to experiment, try these blends:

- Rice Flour + Tapioca Starch + Potato Starch: Creates a light and chewy texture.

- Coconut Flour + Almond Flour: Offers a balance of moisture absorption and softness.
- Chickpea Flour + Cornmeal: Adds a nutty flavor and firm texture.

Conclusion: Embracing Gluten-Free and Low-Carb Creativity

Gluten-free and low-carb pizzas prove that dietary restrictions don't have to limit flavor or creativity. From the crispiness of cauliflower crust to the rich indulgence of cheese-based crusts, these recipes offer delicious alternatives for everyone to enjoy. By mastering the techniques and ingredients outlined in this chapter, you'll be able to create satisfying pizzas that cater to a variety of dietary needs.

In the next chapter, we'll explore the art of pairing pizzas with beverages, diving into the perfect wines, beers, and non-alcoholic drinks to enhance your pizza experience. Let's continue celebrating the endless possibilities of pizza!

Chapter 14: Troubleshooting Pizza Problems

Even the most experienced pizza makers encounter challenges in their pursuit of the perfect pie. From soggy crusts to uneven cooking and bland flavors, these problems can derail your efforts and leave you frustrated. The good news is that every issue has a solution. By understanding the causes of common pizza problems and learning how to address them, you can elevate your pizza-making skills and achieve consistently excellent results.

In this chapter, we'll explore the most common pizza-making issues, offer practical tips for avoiding pitfalls, and discuss how to adjust your techniques for different ovens, climates, and ingredients.

Common Pizza Problems and How to Solve Them

1. Soggy Crusts

A soggy crust is one of the most frequent complaints among pizza enthusiasts. The ideal crust should be crisp and firm, providing a sturdy base for toppings.

Causes:

- Too much moisture in the dough or toppings.
- Baking at a low temperature.
- Overloading the pizza with heavy ingredients.

Solutions:

1. Use a Pizza Stone or Steel: These tools retain and distribute heat evenly, ensuring a crisp bottom crust. Preheat for at least 30 minutes at the oven's highest setting.

2. Pre-Bake the Crust: Par-bake your dough for 5-7 minutes before adding toppings to prevent sogginess.

3. Drain Toppings: Remove excess moisture from ingredients like tomatoes, mushrooms, or mozzarella by patting them dry or roasting them beforehand.

4. Increase Oven Temperature: Bake at 500°F or higher for a shorter time to achieve a crisp crust.

2. Uneven Cooking

Unevenly cooked pizzas, where the crust is burnt but the center is undercooked, are a common issue.

Causes:

- Uneven heat distribution in the oven.
- Dough thickness inconsistencies.
- Placing the pizza too close to the heating element.

Solutions:

1. Use a Pizza Stone or Steel: These tools help even out heat and ensure consistent cooking.
2. Rotate the Pizza: Turn the pizza halfway through baking to expose all sides to equal heat.
3. Adjust Rack Position: Place the pizza on the middle rack for optimal heat exposure.
4. Roll Dough Evenly: Ensure your dough is of consistent thickness, with no thick or thin spots.

3. Bland Flavors

A bland pizza can ruin the entire experience. Each component—crust, sauce, cheese, and toppings—should contribute to the overall flavor.

Causes:

- Under-seasoned dough, sauce, or toppings.
- Poor-quality ingredients.
- Insufficient salt or spices.

Solutions:

1. Season Every Layer: Add salt, garlic, herbs, or spices to the dough, sauce, and toppings.
2. Invest in Quality Ingredients: Use high-quality cheeses, tomatoes, and fresh herbs for better flavor.
3. Experiment with Bold Flavors: Add a drizzle of olive oil, a sprinkle of Parmesan, or fresh basil leaves after baking.

4. Burnt Crust or Toppings

Burnt spots on your pizza can result from high heat or overcooking.

Causes:

- Leaving the pizza in the oven for too long.
- Using too much flour on the bottom of the dough, which can burn.
- Baking too close to the heating element.

Solutions:

1. Watch the Baking Time: Keep an eye on your pizza and remove it as soon as the crust is golden and the cheese is bubbling.

2. Use Cornmeal or Parchment Paper: These alternatives to flour prevent sticking without burning.

3. Adjust Oven Racks: Place the pizza further from the heating element to avoid excessive charring.

5. Dough Issues

From sticky dough that's hard to handle to tough crusts that lack elasticity, dough problems are common but fixable.

Causes:

- Improper hydration levels.
- Over-kneading or under-kneading.
- Insufficient proofing time.

Solutions:

1. Balance Hydration: Follow the recommended water-to-flour ratio and adjust for humidity.

2. Knead Correctly: Knead until the dough is smooth and elastic but not overly firm.

3. Allow Adequate Proofing: Let the dough rise for the recommended time to develop flavor and texture.

6. Cheese Issues

Cheese can melt unevenly, release excess oil, or fail to achieve the desired gooey texture.

Causes:

- Using low-quality cheese.

- Overbaking or baking at too high a temperature.
- Improper layering of toppings.

Solutions:

1. Choose High-Quality Cheese: Use fresh mozzarella or a blend of cheeses for better melting properties.
2. Add Cheese Midway Through Baking: To prevent overcooking, sprinkle cheese halfway through the baking process.
3. Layer Cheese Wisely: Place cheese beneath some toppings to protect it from direct heat.

Tips for Improving Your Pizza-Making Skills

1. Practice Dough Handling
   - Use a floured surface to prevent sticking.
   - Roll or stretch the dough evenly for consistent cooking.
2. Experiment with Oven Settings
   - If your oven doesn't reach high temperatures, preheat for longer or use the broil setting for the last minute of baking.
3. Prep Ingredients Properly
   - Slice toppings thinly to ensure even cooking.
   - Roast or sauté certain ingredients, like mushrooms or onions, to enhance flavor.
4. Test Different Flours
   - Experiment with bread flour for a chewier crust or whole wheat flour for a nuttier flavor.
5. Learn from Mistakes
   - Keep notes on what works and what doesn't to refine your technique over time.

Adjusting for Different Ovens and Climates

1. Adapting to Ovens
   - Conventional Ovens: Use a pizza stone or steel for high heat retention.
   - Convection Ovens: Reduce baking time slightly due to circulating heat.

- Outdoor Pizza Ovens: Monitor closely, as they reach higher temperatures and cook faster.

2. Accounting for Climate

- Humidity: In humid climates, reduce the dough's water content slightly to avoid sticky dough.

- Altitude: In high-altitude areas, increase hydration and reduce yeast for better dough performance.

Quick Fixes for Common Problems

1. Soggy Crust: Pre-bake the dough and use drier toppings.

2. Burnt Toppings: Add sensitive ingredients like basil or arugula after baking.

3. Rubbery Cheese: Use fresh mozzarella and add it midway through baking.

4. Cracking Dough: Allow the dough to rest and avoid over-kneading.

Conclusion: Mastering the Art of Troubleshooting

Pizza-making is as much about problem-solving as it is about creativity. By understanding the causes of common issues and implementing the solutions in this chapter, you can overcome obstacles and perfect your technique. Whether you're dealing with soggy crusts, uneven cooking, or bland flavors, these tips will help you achieve consistently delicious results.

In the next chapter, we'll explore the art of pairing pizzas with complementary beverages, diving into the perfect wines, beers, and non-alcoholic options to enhance your pizza experience. Let's continue mastering the craft of pizza-making!

Chapter 15: Hosting the Perfect Pizza Night

Hosting a pizza night is more than just making and eating delicious pies—it's about creating a fun, interactive experience that brings people together. Whether it's a casual family dinner, a festive gathering with friends, or a themed party, pizza nights are the perfect way to celebrate food, creativity, and community. With a little planning, you can craft an unforgettable evening featuring a pizza buffet with multiple toppings and crusts, expertly paired beverages, and activities that encourage everyone to get involved.

In this chapter, we'll guide you through everything you need to host the ultimate pizza night. From setting up a pizza buffet and pairing your creations with complementary wines and beers to organizing fun activities like make-your-own stations, you'll find all the tips and tricks to make your event a smashing success.

Why Pizza Nights Are a Crowd-Pleaser

1. Customization for Everyone

Pizza's versatility ensures there's something for every guest, from classic Margherita lovers to those craving creative, gourmet flavors.

2. Interactive and Engaging

Building pizzas together is a hands-on activity that sparks conversation and creativity, making it ideal for family and friends.

3. Casual Yet Special

Pizza nights can be as laid-back or as sophisticated as you want, adapting to any occasion.

Setting the Scene for Pizza Night

1. Planning Your Space

- Workstations: Set up multiple stations for dough preparation, topping assembly, and baking to ensure smooth workflow.

- Seating: Arrange seating for dining, but also provide standing areas near the pizza-making station for mingling.

- Ambience: Use string lights, candles, or pizza-themed décor to set the mood.

2. Prepping the Essentials

- Oven or Grill: Ensure your oven, pizza stone, or outdoor pizza oven is preheated and ready to go.

- Tools: Stock up on pizza peels, cutters, and rolling pins to streamline the process.

- Serving Plates: Provide plenty of serving boards or trays for presenting the pizzas.

Creating a Pizza Buffet

The centerpiece of your pizza night is the pizza buffet, where guests can explore a variety of crusts, sauces, and toppings. Here's how to organize it for maximum enjoyment.

1. Crust Options

- Classic Dough: For traditionalists.
- Whole Wheat Dough: Adds a nutty, wholesome flavor.
- Gluten-Free Crusts: Like cauliflower or almond flour for dietary needs.
- Pre-Baked Flatbreads: A quick, ready-to-use option.

2. Sauces

Offer a range of sauces to cater to different tastes:

- Traditional Tomato Sauce: A staple for classic pizzas.
- White Sauce: Creamy and indulgent for gourmet pies.
- Pesto: Herbaceous and nutty for a fresh twist.
- Specialty Sauces: Like BBQ, spicy marinara, or garlic olive oil.

3. Toppings

Divide toppings into categories for easy selection:

- Cheeses: Mozzarella, Parmesan, goat cheese, feta, vegan cheese.
- Proteins: Pepperoni, sausage, grilled chicken, tofu, plant-based meats.
- Vegetables: Bell peppers, mushrooms, onions, olives, spinach, arugula.

- Premium Add-Ons: Fresh basil, truffle oil, caramelized onions, roasted garlic.

4. Finishing Touches

- Herbs: Fresh parsley, oregano, or cilantro.
- Drizzles: Olive oil, balsamic reduction, or hot honey.
- Seasonings: Red pepper flakes, sea salt, cracked black pepper.

Pairing Pizzas with Beverages

Drinks can elevate the flavors of your pizzas. Offer a variety of options to suit your guests' preferences.

1. Wines
- Light Reds: Pair well with tomato-based pizzas (e.g., Pinot Noir, Chianti).
- White Wines: Crisp whites like Sauvignon Blanc complement veggie-heavy pizzas.
- Sparkling Wines: Prosecco adds a celebratory touch and balances rich flavors.

2. Beers
- Pale Ales: Work with tangy, spicy pizzas.
- Stouts: Great for meaty or BBQ-based pizzas.
- Lagers: A neutral option that pairs with most flavors.

3. Non-Alcoholic Options
- Mocktails: Create a basil lemonade or sparkling berry soda.
- Iced Tea or Lemonade: Refreshing for guests of all ages.
- Sparkling Water: Serve with lemon or lime for a simple, elegant touch.

Fun Activities for Pizza Night

1. Make-Your-Own Pizza Stations
- How It Works: Provide dough, sauces, toppings, and tools for guests to assemble their own pizzas.
- Customization: Offer gluten-free and vegan options to cater to dietary restrictions.

- Supervise Baking: Designate someone to manage the oven to ensure even cooking.

2. Pizza-Making Contests

- Categories: Most creative topping combination, best presentation, or fastest assembly.

- Prizes: Award small prizes like recipe books, aprons, or pizza cutters.

3. Themed Nights

- Regional Themes: Italian classics, New York-style, or Mediterranean-inspired pizzas.

- Holiday Themes: Create Halloween pizzas with olive "spiders" or heart-shaped Valentine's pies.

4. Kids' Corner

- Mini Pizzas: Provide smaller dough portions for kids to craft their own creations.

- Decorating Fun: Let them "paint" their pizzas with sauces and toppings.

Sides and Accompaniments

Pair your pizzas with complementary sides to round out the meal.

1. Appetizers

- Garlic Knots: Warm, buttery, and perfect for dipping.

- Caprese Salad: A fresh, light starter.

- Antipasto Platter: Include cured meats, cheeses, olives, and marinated vegetables.

2. Salads

- Caesar Salad: A classic pairing with pizza.

- Arugula Salad: Tossed with lemon vinaigrette for a peppery contrast.

3. Desserts

- Dessert Pizzas: Nutella and banana, s'mores, or fruit tart pizzas.

- Gelato or Ice Cream: Offer a cool, creamy finish to the meal.

Tips for a Successful Pizza Night

1. Prepare Ahead

- Pre-make dough and sauces to reduce stress.
- Pre-chop toppings and arrange them in bowls for easy access.

2. Test Your Oven

- Practice baking a pizza beforehand to determine optimal settings and times.

3. Involve Guests

- Encourage everyone to participate in the pizza-making process.

4. Keep It Flexible

- Offer options for dietary restrictions and preferences.

Conclusion: A Celebration of Community and Creativity

A pizza night is more than just a meal—it's an opportunity to bring people together, spark creativity, and share a memorable experience. With a well-organized pizza buffet, perfectly paired drinks, and engaging activities, you can create an event that leaves your guests raving. Whether you're hosting a casual family gathering or an elaborate party, the tips and ideas in this chapter will help you pull off the perfect pizza night.

As you wrap up your pizza journey, remember that pizza-making is about experimenting, having fun, and enjoying the process. Every slice tells a story, and every gathering celebrates the universal love for this timeless dish. Let the pizzas keep coming and the memories keep growing!

Conclusion: A Lifelong Love for Pizza

Pizza isn't just food—it's a celebration of creativity, tradition, and community. Across the globe, it has been reimagined in countless ways, from the classic Margherita of Naples to modern dessert pizzas adorned with chocolate and fruit. This book has explored the rich world of pizza-making, offering techniques, recipes, and inspiration to help you craft the perfect pie at home. Whether you're a novice or an experienced cook, this journey was designed to deepen your appreciation for pizza and equip you with the skills to make it your own.

As we conclude, let's revisit the key lessons shared throughout this book, encourage you to continue experimenting, and celebrate the endless possibilities of homemade pizza.

The Craft of Pizza-Making

Mastering the Basics

Every great pizza begins with mastering its core elements. These fundamentals form the foundation of your pizza-making journey:

1. The Dough:

- Learning to knead, proof, and stretch dough is essential.

- Recipes for classic, gluten-free, and low-carb crusts offered you diverse options to suit any preference or dietary need.

2. The Sauce:

- From rich tomato sauces to creamy white sauces and bold pestos, the sauce is the flavor backbone of a great pizza.

- Techniques for balancing acidity, sweetness, and seasoning ensure a perfect complement to your toppings.

3. The Cheese:

- Understanding the melting properties and flavor profiles of different cheeses helps you create pizzas with gooey textures and robust flavors.

- Exploring vegan alternatives broadened your ability to cater to dietary restrictions.

4. The Oven:

- Whether you're using a home oven, pizza stone, outdoor pizza oven, or grill, temperature control and heat distribution are key.

Building on the Basics

Once you've mastered the foundations, the real fun begins—experimenting with toppings, styles, and creative twists. This book introduced you to:

1. Classic Recipes:

- Traditional Italian pizzas like Margherita and Quattro Formaggi celebrated the beauty of simplicity.

2. Global Inspirations:

- Recipes like Thai chicken pizza, Indian tikka pizza, and Middle Eastern za'atar pizza showed how to infuse international flavors into your creations.

3. Specialty Options:

- Gluten-free, low-carb, vegetarian, and vegan pizzas proved that dietary adaptations can still deliver bold, satisfying flavors.

4. Dessert Pizzas:

- Sweet creations like Nutella and banana pizza or fruit tart pizza pushed the boundaries of what pizza can be.

The Joy of Experimentation

Pizza-making is an art, not a science. The beauty lies in its versatility—you can adapt every recipe to reflect your tastes, preferences, and creativity. Here's how to keep evolving as a pizza maker:

1. Play with Flavors

- Experiment with sweet, salty, and spicy combinations.

- Add unexpected ingredients like fruits, herbs, or exotic spices to surprise your taste buds.

2. Try New Techniques

- Explore sourdough starters for your crust or try grilling pizza for a smoky flavor.

- Invest in tools like a pizza steel or outdoor oven to elevate your results.

3. Celebrate Seasonality

- Let seasonal ingredients guide your toppings—roasted squash in the fall, fresh tomatoes and basil in the summer.

4. Learn from Mistakes

- Every burned crust or soggy center is a lesson. Embrace these moments as opportunities to refine your craft.

The Community of Pizza

Pizza is inherently social. It's a dish meant to be shared, bringing people together in ways few foods can. Hosting pizza nights, as discussed in Chapter 15, is a wonderful way to bond with loved ones. It encourages collaboration, creativity, and connection.

Pizza and Memories

- Pizza often evokes nostalgia: the neighborhood pizzeria of your childhood, late-night slices with friends, or homemade pies on a rainy afternoon.

- By making pizza at home, you're not just creating food—you're creating moments that will be remembered and cherished.

Key Takeaways from This Journey

Let's recap the invaluable techniques, recipes, and tips shared throughout this book:

1. Perfecting the Basics:

- Dough, sauce, cheese, and toppings each play a crucial role in the final product.

2. Exploring Creativity:

- From global flavors to dessert pizzas, the possibilities are endless.

3. Troubleshooting:

- Addressing common pizza problems ensures every pie turns out beautifully.

4. Hosting and Sharing:

- Pizza-making is an experience meant to be shared with others, whether through make-your-own stations or pairing pizzas with drinks and sides.

Embracing Pizza as a Lifelong Journey

The world of pizza is vast, and this book is just the beginning. Whether you're a fan of thin-crust Neapolitan pizzas or thick, cheesy deep-dish creations, there's always something new to discover. Embrace pizza-making as a lifelong journey—one where every pie tells a story and every recipe is an opportunity to learn and grow.

Inspiration for Your Next Steps

1. Dive Deeper into Regional Styles:

- Explore the nuances of Chicago deep-dish, Detroit square, or Roman-style pizzas.

2. Master Advanced Techniques:

- Experiment with sourdough fermentation, wood-fired ovens, or unique baking methods.

3. Teach Others:

- Share your knowledge and passion with friends and family, inspiring them to join the pizza-making adventure.

4. Celebrate Pizza Day:

- Dedicate a weekly pizza night to continue refining your skills and trying new recipes.

A Final Word of Encouragement

Pizza is more than just a dish—it's an invitation to be creative, to connect with others, and to enjoy the process of making something truly delicious. Every time you roll out dough, sprinkle cheese, and slide a pizza into the oven, you're participating in a tradition that spans centuries and continents.

So, whether you're a seasoned pizza maker or just beginning your journey, keep experimenting, keep sharing, and keep celebrating the magic of pizza.

Remember: the perfect pie is always within reach, and the joy of pizza-making is as endless as the topping combinations you can imagine.

Thank you for embarking on this pizza journey. May your crusts always be crisp, your toppings flavorful, and your pizza nights filled with laughter and love. Now, go forth and create your masterpiece—one slice at a time!

Don't miss out!

Visit the website below and you can sign up to receive emails whenever Olivia Bennett publishes a new book. There's no charge and no obligation.

https://books2read.com/r/B-A-QLEKD-OKGAG

About the Author

Olivia Bennett is a celebrated food writer and chef with expertise spanning multiple culinary disciplines. With a passion for making home cooking accessible, she specializes in guiding readers through everything from hearty casseroles to delicate pastries. Her work is known for its clear instructions, practical tips, and deep understanding of both traditional and modern cooking techniques.

www.ingramcontent.com/pod-product-compliance
Lightning Source LLC
LaVergne TN
LVHW090124160826
845673LV00015B/838

* 9 7 9 8 2 3 0 1 6 6 4 4 3 *